MSP®
OGC Portfolio Product

Fundamentals of Benefit Realization

London: TSO

TSO
information & publishing solutions

Published by TSO (The Stationery Office) and available from:

Online
www.tsoshop.co.uk

Mail, Telephone, Fax & E-mail
TSO
PO Box 29, Norwich, NR3 1GN
Telephone orders/General enquiries: 0870 600 5522
Fax orders: 0870 600 5533
E-mail: customer.services@tso.co.uk
Textphone: 0870 240 3701

TSO@Blackwell and other Accredited Agents

Customers can also order publications from:
TSO Ireland
16 Arthur Street, Belfast BT1 4GD
Tel: 028 9023 8451 Fax: 028 9023 5401

© The Stationery Office 2010

All rights reserved. No part of this publication may be reproduced, stored in a retrieval system, or transmitted in any form or by any means, electronic, mechanical, photocopying, recording or otherwise without the permission of the publisher.

Copyright in the typographical arrangement and design is vested in The Stationery Office Limited.

Applications for reproduction should be made in writing to The Stationery Office Limited, St Crispins, Duke Street, Norwich NR3 1PD.

No liability is accepted for any loss resulting from use of or reliance on this content. While every effort is made to ensure the accuracy and reliability of the information, TSO cannot accept responsibility for errors, omissions or inaccuracies.

Gerald Bradley has asserted his moral rights under the Copyright, Designs and Patents Act 1988, to be identified as the author of this work.

Extracts from Benefits Realisation Management 2nd edition 2010 have been reproduced with kind permission of Gower Publishing

The Swirl logo™ is a Trade Mark of the Office of Government Commerce

MSP® is a Registered Trade Mark of the Office of Government Commerce in the United Kingdom and other countries

PRINCE® is a Registered Trade Mark of the Office of Government Commerce in the United Kingdom and other countries

PRINCE2™ is a Trade Mark of the Office of Government Commerce

P3O® is a Registered Trade Mark of the Office of Government Commerce

A CIP catalogue record for this book is available from the British Library

A Library of Congress CIP catalogue record has been applied for

First published 2010

ISBN 9780113312597

Printed in the United Kingdom by The Stationery Office, London

P002367107   c10   09/10

Contents

List of figures and tables vi

Preface viii

Acknowledgements x

PART 1: FOUNDATIONS FOR BENEFIT REALIZATION 1

1 The importance and value of benefit realization 3
   1.1 Achieving an organization's mission or end goal 3
   1.2 Benefit realization management 3
   1.3 The purpose and scope of BRM 4
   1.4 Scoping the investment 5
   1.5 Effective business change 6
   1.6 Why BRM is of increasing importance 6
   1.7 A compelling investment 8
   1.8 When should BRM be applied? 9

2 Requirements for effective benefit realization 10
   2.1 First things first 10
   2.2 Quality communication 12
   2.3 The centrality of BRM to effective change 12
   2.4 The need for a standard approach 12
   2.5 Stakeholder engagement 13
   2.6 The importance of non-financial benefits 14
   2.7 Critical success factors for effective benefit realization 14

3 The BRM process 15
   3.1 Process essentials 15
   3.2 Characteristics and implications of this lifecycle 16
   3.3 Gateways and reviews 17
   3.4 Flexibility and value of the process 18

PART 2: APPLYING BRM TO PROGRAMMES AND PROJECTS 19

4 Applying BRM Phase 1: set vision and objectives 21
   4.1 The starting point 21
   4.2 Workshop to define and map objectives 21
   4.3 Further analysis and documentation 24

5 Applying BRM Phase 2: identify benefits and changes 28
   5.1 Phase overview 28
   5.2 Analysing and engaging stakeholders 28
   5.3 Benefit identification and mapping 29
   5.4 Developing a benefit distribution matrix 33
   5.5 Requirements definition 33
   5.6 Identifying and consolidating duplicate entities 36
   5.7 Identifying measures for the benefits 36
   5.8 Phase documents 37
   5.9 Resource requirements 39

Contents

6 Applying BRM Phase 3: define initiatives — 40
  6.1 Phase content and process — 40
  6.2 Engaging stakeholders — 40
  6.3 Finalizing and costing requirements — 40
  6.4 Validating, valuing and tracking benefits — 44
  6.5 Developing the benefit realization plan — 47
  6.6 Developing the programme definition document — 47
  6.7 Developing the business case — 48
  6.8 Securing funding — 48
  6.9 Mobilizing resources — 49

7 Applying BRM Phase 4: optimize initiatives — 50
  7.1 Phase overview — 50
  7.2 Stakeholder engagement — 50
  7.3 Checking alignment, internal consistency and balance — 50
  7.4 Optimizing the solution — 54
  7.5 Promoting the BRP — 55
  7.6 Establishing benefit tracking and reporting — 55
  7.7 Resource requirements — 56

8 Applying BRM Phase 5: manage initiatives — 57
  8.1 Foundations for change — 57
  8.2 Roles and responsibilities — 57
  8.3 Overcoming resistance to change — 58
  8.4 Transition into business as usual — 60

9 Applying BRM Phase 6: manage performance — 61
  9.1 Benefit tracking — 61
  9.2 Acting on missed targets — 61
  9.3 Capturing lessons learned — 61
  9.4 Closing the programme — 61

PART 3: ELABORATION OF KEY TECHNIQUES AND RESPONSIBILITIES — 63

10 Definition, classification and validation of benefits — 65
  10.1 Definitions – benefits and related entities — 65
  10.2 Benefit classification — 66
  10.3 Benefit validation — 71
  10.4 Benefit valuation — 71

11 Roles and responsibilities — 73
  11.1 Accountability for benefit realization — 73
  11.2 Portfolio management — 73
  11.3 Programme management — 74
  11.4 Project management — 77

12 Mapping — 79
  12.1 The importance of mapping — 79
  12.2 Types of map — 80
  12.3 Weighting the paths of the maps — 84

13 Measuring — 89
  13.1 The purpose of measuring — 89
  13.2 Definitions and measure attributes — 89
  13.3 Measure attributes and categories — 90
  13.4 Characteristics of good measures — 91
  13.5 Choosing which benefits to measure — 92
  13.6 Responsibilities — 94
  13.7 Tracking and reporting — 95

14 Documentation — 97
  14.1 The purpose of documents — 97
  14.2 Range of documents and relationship between them — 97

PART 4: STRATEGIC ORGANIZATION-WIDE CONSIDERATIONS 101

15 Portfolio management 103
15.1 The scope and purpose of portfolio management 103
15.2 Creating an environment in which a change portfolio will flourish 103
15.3 Active management of the portfolio of change 104
15.4 Responsibility for portfolio management 105
15.5 Getting started 107

16 Embedding BRM within an organization 108
16.1 The need to embed BRM 108
16.2 The process of embedding 108
16.3 Applying BRM to the embedding process 109

17 Case study: the British Council 111
17.1 Introduction 111
17.2 The background 111
17.3 Back to the drawing board 111
17.4 Lighting fires 112
17.5 Mapping at a strategic level 112
17.6 Taking the benefits initiative 112
17.7 What did we learn? 113
17.8 The future 113

Further information 117

Glossary 118

Index 125

List of figures and tables

Figures

Figure 1.1 Focus on the real goal – the end point
Figure 1.2 Why BRM is of increasing importance
Figure 1.3 ROI of BRM based on start time
Figure 2.1 Cart before the horse
Figure 2.2 Framework for success
Figure 2.3 BRM – key driver for change
Figure 3.1 The six phases of the change lifecycle
Figure 4.1 Strategy map for embedding BRM within an organization
Figure 4.2 Strategy map with bounding objectives and programme boundary
Figure 4.3 Linking objectives to a vision
Figure 4.4 Alignment of programme and business objectives
Figure 4.5 Programme categorization by business impact (the Cranfield Grid)
Figure 5.1 Representation of stakeholders and their grouping hierarchy
Figure 5.2 The relationship between different types of benefit
Figure 5.3 Examples of different types of benefit
Figure 5.4 End benefits for different objectives
Figure 5.5 Example benefits map for reducing a carbon footprint
Figure 5.6 Benefits and disbenefits of BRM by stakeholder
Figure 5.7 Example BDM for reducing a carbon footprint
Figure 6.1 Template for a stakeholder profile
Figure 6.2 Generic benefits map with weightings and scores
Figure 6.3 Template for a benefit profile
Figure 6.4 Measure baselines and predictions
Figure 7.1 Misalignment of investment and benefit classifications
Figure 8.1 Overcoming stakeholder resistance
Figure 10.1 Sigma value types
Figure 10.2 Partial benefits map to consider the impact of fewer steps in a process
Figure 11.1 Typical programme structure
Figure 11.2 Alternative organizational structure (for large programmes)
Figure 12.1 Bridging the abyss
Figure 12.2 The centrality of the BDM
Figure 12.3 Strategy map to consider homeworking to grow a business on its current site
Figure 12.4 Benefits map for the objective 'to increase staff productivity'
Figure 12.5 A BDM for the objective 'to increase overall staff productivity'

List of figures and tables | vii

Figure 12.6 Linked weighted generic maps for objectives and benefits
Figure 12.7 Change to benefit relationships
Figure 12.8 Weighted and scored BDM for improving theatre utilization
Figure 13.1 Benefit-measure contributions
Figure 13.2 Benefits map for the objective 'to increase sales revenue'
Figure 13.3 Measure reporting – planned and actual – by stakeholder
Figure 13.4 BRAG report (benefits map one year after implementation)
Figure 14.1 Common documents grouped by theme and phase
Figure 14.2 Common documents grouped by theme and phase (tabular version)
Figure 14.3 Change process with key review documents
Figure 15.1 Structure for a portfolio of programmes and projects
Figure 16.1 Activity themes for embedding BRM within an organization
Figure 16.2 BDM for objective 'to increase programme ROIs'

Tables

Table 7.1 IAM showing benefits by value type and business impact
Table 7.2 IAM showing benefits by beneficiary and by business impact
Table 7.3 IAM showing benefits by change type and value type
Table 7.4 Relationship between enabler features and benefits

Preface

This publication is an easy-to-use practical guide to the realization of benefits (financial and non-financial) from an organization's investment in change.

This publication covers portfolio, programme and project management, although the majority of the guidance relates particularly to programmes.

The text is heavily based on my own practical experience of benefit realization, gained over 20 years as chairman of Sigma, a niche consultancy specializing in benefit realization. It draws on the insights of many of Sigma's consultants, other recognized practitioners in the field, and other recently published documents on the subject.

With its emphasis on programmes, the content of this publication is very closely aligned to the guidance of the Office of Government Commerce (OGC) in *Managing Successful Programmes* (published by the Stationery Office in 2007, and referred to hereafter as MSP®). It seeks to amplify and clarify MSP® guidance on benefit realization.

This publication has been reviewed by a number of experienced benefit realization practitioners from a cross-section of organizations. Many of these reviewers also have considerable experience of relevant related disciplines including:

- Portfolio management
- Portfolio and/or programme management offices (PMOs)
- Programme management
- Project management
- Business change
- OGC's Gateway review process

The publication is divided into four parts:

- **Part 1 Foundations for benefit realization** considers its growing importance, critical success factors, fundamental terminology and a proven process – benefit realization management (BRM)
- **Part 2 Applying BRM to programmes and projects** is a step-by-step description of the process, suitable for both experienced practitioners and those new to benefit realization
- **Part 3 Elaboration of key techniques and responsibilities** is for those who have worked through parts one and two, or for more experienced BRM practitioners
- **Part 4 Strategic organization-wide considerations** covers portfolio management and embedding BRM within an organization, and includes a complete case study.

Part 1 lays the foundations for applying BRM and is suitable for everyone who needs to understand the value and implications of BRM without needing to know how to apply it – including directors, senior managers and senior responsible owners (SROs).

The step-by-step process in Part 2 is suitable for anyone who needs to apply it. It has been kept as concise as possible so as not to inhibit newcomers to BRM. Some of the key techniques are described in more detail in Part 3.

Part 3 is suitable for those with some understanding or experience of BRM. It can be read directly after Part 1, although a quick read of Part 2 is recommended in order to provide a meaningful context for the more sophisticated techniques explored in Part 3.

The final section, Part 4, is appropriate for those with interests or responsibilities beyond programmes or projects, and is particularly relevant to those with strategic, organizational and portfolio interests.

My hope is that this publication will help raise the profile of benefits and provide a simple and practical guide to the successful realization of all types of benefit. It aims to amplify the benefit guidance contained in MSP, incorporate recent relevant academic thinking, and ensure cohesion and consistency. In doing so, it draws heavily from practical experience.

This guide seeks to help people at all levels of experience, but benefit realization is very challenging and requires determination, commitment and significant skills. No publication, however good, would be able to produce BRM experts overnight.

For further information visit the Sigma website, www.sigma-uk.com, and view 'frequently asked questions' (by searching the site for FAQs) or download communication tools, BRM process diagrams and templates. Alternatively, email me at gerald@sigma-uk.com or geraldbradley@talktalk.net.

Acknowledgements

The Stationery Office (TSO) and the author would like to thank Sigma for providing many of the examples and illustrations used in this publication, and Gower Publishing for its kind permission to reproduce extracts from the second edition of Gerald Bradley's *Benefits Realisation Management* (Gower Publishing, 2010).

In addition, TSO and Gerald Bradley would like to thank Barbara Stock and Vanessa Everett from the British Council's centre of excellence for programme and project management for providing the case study, and to the following individuals for their help in reviewing this publication.

REVIEWERS

Peter Clark	Senior Gateway reviewer and review team leader
Emma Dolman	Ministry of Defence
Tim Ellis	Royal Borough of Kensington and Chelsea
Richard Muirhead	Cheshire Constabulary
Howard Overy	COLT Technologies
Andrew Schuster	Department of Health
Barbara Stock	British Council

Part 1
Foundations for benefit realization

1 The importance and value of benefit realization

1.1 ACHIEVING AN ORGANIZATION'S MISSION OR END GOAL

In its broadest sense, benefit realization is about optimizing the flow of benefits from an organization's investment in change. This optimization should ensure that the most appropriate benefits are sought in line with an organization's vision or strategy, and that they are delivered in the most effective way.

Benefit realization thinking is necessary to shape an organization's portfolio of change initiatives, particularly its programmes and projects. The tools and techniques of benefit realization are needed to scope each initiative and to subsequently ensure that the expected benefits are achieved.

For an organization to become successful and then to maintain this position in a challenging economic environment, benefit realization is of fundamental importance. All investment in change must support the organization's strategy and deliver a substantial and demonstrable return on investment (ROI). So, for any organization, there is little that can be more important or more urgent.

Although benefit realization, defined in this way, is achievable, it is extremely challenging and is far from automatic. It requires:

- Serious commitment at all levels of management, but particularly at the most senior level.
- Funding, resources and experienced skills.
- A proven process. The process described in this publication – benefit realization management (BRM) – is such a process.

1.2 BENEFIT REALIZATION MANAGEMENT

In the 1970s I was working for BP as a project manager. I was aware that many techniques were being developed to improve the management of the project, usually the delivery of the IT system, but that little attention was being given to managing the business change and almost no attention to managing the benefits. Projects were generally considered successful if the technology was delivered to specification, preferably on time and within budget. Tracing impact on business performance was sketchy or non-existent.

So, in the 1980s, I introduced the idea of managing benefits, including the term 'benefit management', and started to develop an approach with appropriate tools and techniques. In 1986 I left BP and set up Sigma to share this approach with other organizations and provide consultancy services to help them apply the approach to projects, programmes and portfolios.

The term 'benefit management' was in common use until 2003 when it changed to 'benefit realization management'. This change happened for two main reasons:

- Some people were confusing benefit management with the management of personnel benefits such as salaries, cars and pensions
- There was a desire to increase the focus on 'realization', because it is possible to manage benefits and not realize them.

Today, MSP uses both terms interchangeably while other approaches make a distinction between benefit management and benefit realization, considering them two separate parts of an overall process. This publication, in agreement with MSP, sees the process as a continual one and separation into two parts as not helpful. Therefore, the term used throughout this publication is benefit realization management, or BRM. This is a powerful yet flexible process, which has been extensively applied to a wide variety of investments in change, in both public and private sectors, for more than 20 years.

1.3 THE PURPOSE AND SCOPE OF BRM

Benefits are only valuable if they are delivered or realized. The purpose of benefit realization is to maximize the achieved or actual return on investment (AROI) from change, including the realization of the non-financial benefits. The ROI is the number that goes into the business case and sadly often bears little resemblance to the AROI.

BRM is about doing the right things, the right way. All investment in change should realize benefits – those which are agreed as valuable to the organization and its related stakeholders, and are in line with the organization's vision and mission. Spending shareholders' or tax payers' money to satisfy a whim or to fund a pet project should not be on the agenda.

BRM is applicable to all kinds of change and the approach is sophisticated and scalable. A change that involves several of the following characteristics would probably best be managed as a programme, and is likely to require a sophisticated application of BRM:

- It has multiple stakeholders from across the organization
- It has stakeholders from outside the organization that is making the investment
- It includes many disbenefits
- It requires a significant amount of business change
- It embraces cultural change
- It is aiming to realize a broad range of different types of benefit
- It has a long duration
- It has strategic potential for the business
- It requires major investment.

Alternatively, a small project focused on changing technology to respond to new legislation may only require a limited application of BRM techniques.

Example

Several years ago, while I was helping to embed BRM in a pharmaceutical company, the director for drug development mandated that all projects costing over £100,000 should apply BRM. While this was clearly a move in the right direction, I could not understand why BRM should not be applied to all projects if it was suitably scaled.

Furthermore, if there was to be a cut-off for the mandated application of BRM, it should not be based on project cost but on potential benefits – for example, a project costing £90,000 with potential benefits of £1 million needs BRM far more than a project costing £110,000 with potential benefits of £200,000.

1.4 SCOPING THE INVESTMENT

Unfortunately, in many organizations benefits are still an afterthought – the things you get (if you are lucky) when the programme or project delivers. In general, benefits should be the *raison d'être* of change and the starting point for any potential change and the driver at all stages, particularly when scoping and shaping the investment.

It is, therefore, no accident that BRM is an extremely powerful process for scoping change at all levels:

- At strategic or portfolio level
- At programme level
- At project level.

BRM is powerful because it:

- Starts by recognizing or determining where the organization is today (the 'as is')
- Considers the drivers for change – the need to fix problems and exploit opportunities
- Establishes the desired business end goal (the 'to be')
- Determines the changes required to achieve the transition from the 'as is' to the 'to be', once the 'as is' and the 'to be' situations have been defined (see Figure 1.1)

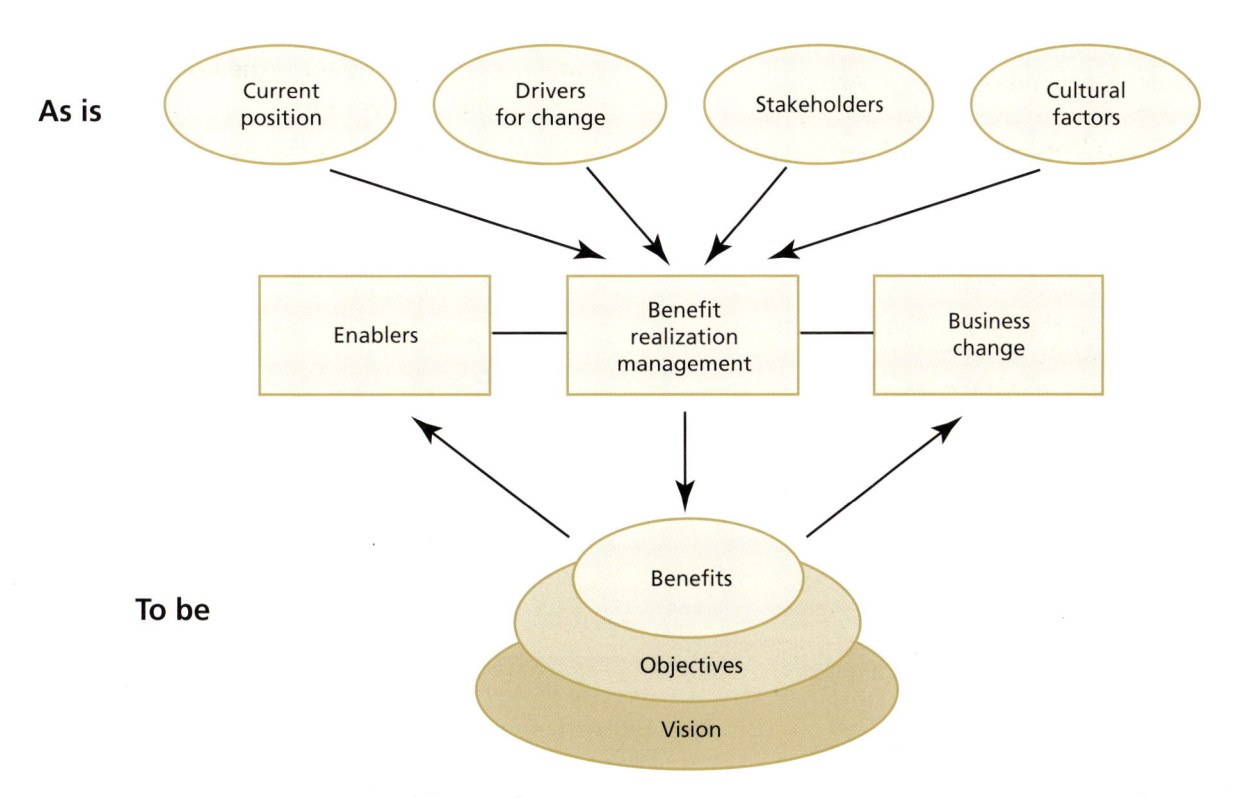

Figure 1.1 Focus on the real goal – the end point

- Monitors and tracks progress towards the end goal, including the realization of benefits
- Performs all of the above through carefully planned engagement of stakeholders.

It is at the scoping stage that BRM can, sometimes significantly, reduce the potential costs of change by focusing investment where it will deliver the greatest value (see the utilities company example). This focus can range from deciding which programmes or projects to invest in, to choosing what enabler features to acquire and implement.

Example

A utilities company was planning to spend about £25 million on technological improvements. To help scope the required changes, Sigma was asked to facilitate a few benefits workshops. One of the consequences of these workshops was recognition by the organization that it could achieve 80% of the desired benefits for an expenditure of £5 million. This was a course it subsequently decided to pursue, thus saving £20 million.

Unfortunately, many organizations do not consider the application of BRM until they have completed at least the high-level, if not the detailed, scoping. By then, they have missed possibly the biggest contribution that BRM can bring. This missed opportunity is often recognized too late.

1.5 EFFECTIVE BUSINESS CHANGE

Benefits are dependent on the successful implementation of the appropriate **change**, where the change is normally the integration of new enablers (e.g. technology, information, processes) with **business changes** (e.g. working practices, behaviours, attitudes). This integration should deliver the required new business state, described in what MSP calls the blueprint.

For more than 50 years the focus of attention has been on the enablers, perhaps because this is where much of the hard cash is consumed. Enablers are invariably specified, developed and implemented, and although this is seldom within budget and timescale, most enablers are eventually delivered. However, without the related business changes the benefits will never be achieved.

For many years business change was largely ignored and benefits were seldom achieved. Even today essential business changes are:

- Frequently not identified
- Not properly costed and budgeted
- Not adequately resourced
- Squeezed for funding, especially when enabler costs overrun
- Not managed with the required dedication and skills.

A key part of BRM is to give due prominence to business change.

1.6 WHY BRM IS OF INCREASING IMPORTANCE

There are many reasons why BRM is of increasing importance today. In the last few years there has been a noticeable increase in the attention given to benefit realization by management at all levels. In particular, the UK government now puts a strong emphasis on benefits, which is being channelled directly to government departments, but also indirectly through the Treasury, the National Audit Office (NAO) and the OGC. In the private sector, chief executives, managing directors and other senior managers are mandating the application of BRM to programmes and projects, demanding increased quality and rigour in business cases and more meaningful benefit tracking and reporting.

This top-level drive has probably arisen as a consequence of two factors:

- In an increasingly challenging global economy, organizations cannot afford to continue wasting costly investment. Organizations must expect benefits from change and ensure that expectations are fulfilled.
- Business environments, both private and public, are increasingly complex and changing rapidly, making benefit realization more difficult. This is evident from a historical perspective.

There has been a progressive change in the development of computing in business over five decades (see Figure 1.2). In the 1960s:

- Most projects were about automating clerical processes (e.g. payroll and accounting) where the main benefit was 'reduced costs'.
- Most projects were initiated and funded by a single department which also managed the change and received the benefits.
- The project team identified the benefits, made the business case if one was required, and oversaw the required changes.
- The automation of clerical processes meant that most benefits would be realized very soon after implementation, and so in the rare cases where organizations required that the realization of the benefits was demonstrated or measured, the project team would still be available to undertake this task.
- The environment was relatively stable. For an 18-month project both the internal and external environments at the end would be similar to what they were at the beginning – so there was far less risk that goalposts would have moved.

Today, on the other hand, the situation is quite different:

- Far more benefits relate to different kinds of added value rather than a simple reduction of costs.
- Projects, and especially programmes, involve multiple stakeholders often going right across an organization and reaching outside to suppliers, partners and many other kinds of related groups.
- Both the nature of the benefits and their delivery vehicles (programmes and projects) are such that the identification of benefits cannot be effectively achieved by the programme or project team. Proactive stakeholder engagement is required to determine a comprehensive set of quality benefits.
- Many benefits will not be realized until months, and sometimes years, after the changes have been implemented, so the programme/project team will not be around to track and report the benefits. The process of measuring and reporting benefits must be adopted by its rightful owner – the business.
- Significant changes, internal and/or external, can occur within six months, highlighting the limited value of a single snapshot such as a cost benefit analysis.

Although the prizes today may be far greater, so are the risks and so is the complexity – hence the need for BRM.

	Driven by	Used by	Opportunity	Benefits
1960s	IT	IT	Automation	**Reduced costs**
1970s	IT	Business	Transaction processing	
1980s	Business	Business and third parties	MIS, systems integration	
1990s	Business and third parties	Business and third parties	EIS, process re-engineering	
2000s	Senior management	Senior management	Knowledge management, teamworking, e-business	**Added value**

Figure 1.2 Why BRM is of increasing importance

1.7 A COMPELLING INVESTMENT

In recent years there have been many studies about the success, or rather the lack of success, of programmes and projects. These have been undertaken by academic bodies, consultancies and government groups such as the NAO and OGC. In essence, they found that:

- Without a structured approach to benefit realization such as BRM, most programmes and projects will achieve between 10% and 25% of potential benefits, with 30% to 40% of projects delivering no benefits at all.
- Only about 35% of organizations are effectively tracking the realization of benefits. This has steadily improved from less than 5% in 1990, but still has a long way to go.

Based on the UK's overall investment in change and the resulting impact using two different measures, I estimate that the cost to the UK for this waste is in excess of £50 billion per annum.

Some companies claim that the application of BRM has increased the AROI from their portfolio of projects from around 20% to 80%. This is often the result of realizing benefits earlier, achieving more of them and sustaining them for longer. A good and achievable target is 80%. To achieve 100% of potential benefits is probably not universally practicable and would, in any case, require enormous and probably unrealistic investment.

Applying BRM to a portfolio, programme or project is an investment. The cost of applying BRM is usually between 4% and 6% of the total programme costs. For a project, the cost may be proportionally higher. If the application of BRM increases the realization of benefits from, say, 20% to 80% then, on the worst kind of investment (i.e. one where the planned benefits only equal the planned costs), the ROI of BRM lies between 1000% and 1500%. If the planned benefits were double the planned costs then the ROI of BRM is also double. Although, in these examples, we are looking at financials, not all programmes will deliver significant financial value.

Very few portfolios will have investments yielding returns of this magnitude, so the application of BRM is surely a no-brainer.

In addition to the return from the improved realization of benefits, BRM can reduce, sometimes substantially, the anticipated project costs, as illustrated by the utilities company example in section 1.4.

1.8 WHEN SHOULD BRM BE APPLIED?

To achieve the maximum return from BRM it needs to be applied from the earliest possible stage (when the idea for change is first floated), although it can still give a healthy, but much smaller, return later in the lifecycle. Figure 1.3 indicates how the ROI changes in relation to the start time for the application of BRM.

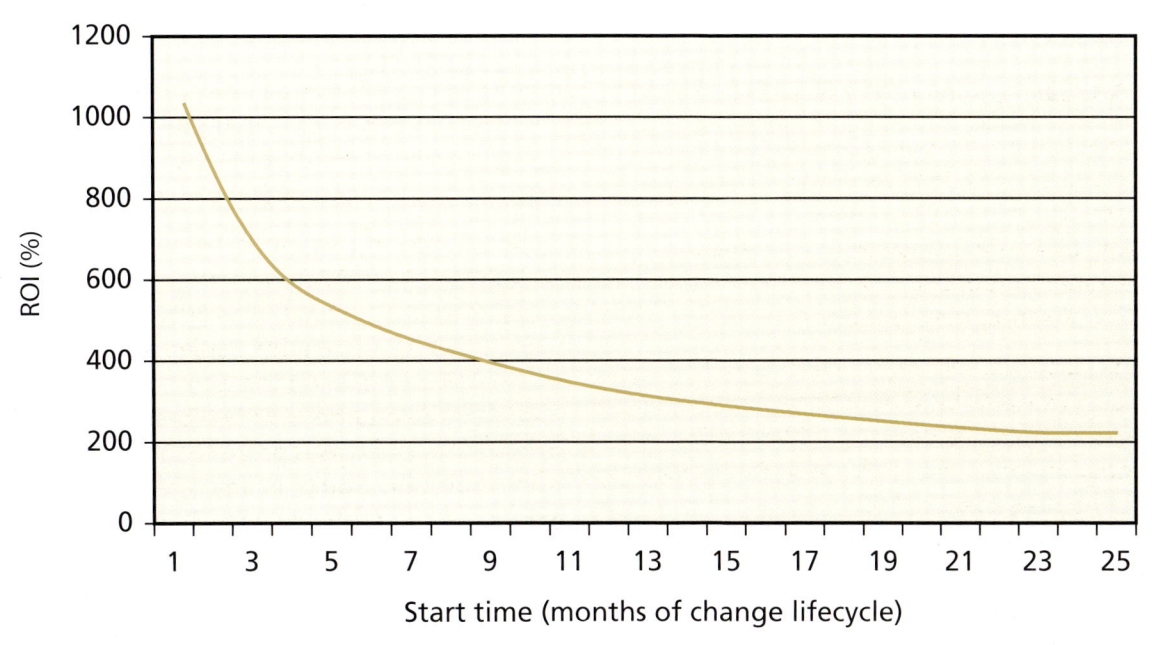

Figure 1.3 ROI of BRM based on start time

2 Requirements for effective benefit realization

2.1 FIRST THINGS FIRST

In general, common sense suggests that you should know where you want to get to before you set out, but this kind of thinking is unfortunately not always evident in project and programme management. It is not unusual to find organizations starting with a solution – a new system and new piece of technology – and then hunting for benefits to justify the investment. This is generally referred to as a 'cart before the horse' mentality (see Figure 2.1).

Three common reasons for the cart before the horse mentality are:

- The enablers (the cart), such as buildings, technology, systems etc., tend to be very physical and tangible and so are easier to focus on than many of the benefits.
- Salespeople and the media sell enablers rather than benefits.
- There is a perception, not always valid, that the major component of expenditure will be associated with the enablers. The business change needed to embed the enablers is often not fully identified or costed.

Although these reasons may be understandable this mindset can often result in disastrous outcomes (see the next example).

For many organizations a fundamental change of culture is required, and this may take several years (see Chapter 16). During this transition a modified version of the process described in this publication may be required.

> **Example**
> A blue-chip multinational invested in a new financial system, to be rolled out across the organization. The focus was on the enabler, the new system, and the IT director was handsomely rewarded for implementing the system on time and within budget. Unfortunately, not everything worked as intended and it was almost five months before the company was able to invoice clients for the products and services it was providing. The company faced bankruptcy. It managed to survive, but at considerable cost.

'To succeed' is a common aim of most individuals and organizations yet there is often no common or shared understanding of what success looks like. For some it may mean delivering the enabler (e.g. the IT system – 'cart before the horse'),

Figure 2.1 Cart before the horse

Requirements for effective benefit realization | **11**

for others the focus will be on satisfying the conditions (e.g. on time and within budget), and for others it will be achieving the ultimate goal – fulfilling the vision or objectives.

The framework depicted in Figure 2.2 (which also highlights the main entities of BRM) can help in the articulation of success and is likely to lead to a more holistic and valuable outcome by:

- Defining where we want to get to
- Determining the best way to get there
- Managing all the changes to get there
- Demonstrating that we have arrived.

Although it may not always be possible to define the destination before setting out, it is generally helpful to start with a reasonable idea of what success looks like. The BRM process, which is flexible and iterative, can then add detail along the way.

'Where you want to get to' is best defined by a vision statement or at least some clear objectives, underpinned by a set of benefits. Deciding upon the best route to success involves:

- Determining the optimum set of enablers and business changes needed to deliver the required benefits. The integration of the enablers and business changes gives a picture of the target future state of the organization – referred to as the blueprint by MSP.

Defining where we want to get to:

Vision   Objectives   Benefits

Determining the best way to get there
Managing all the changes to get there

Acquiring new capabilitites and embedding them within the culture, practices and behaviours of the organization

Enablers   Business changes

Early view of blueprint

Minimizing the impact of disbenefits

Disbenefits

Demonstrating that we have arrived:

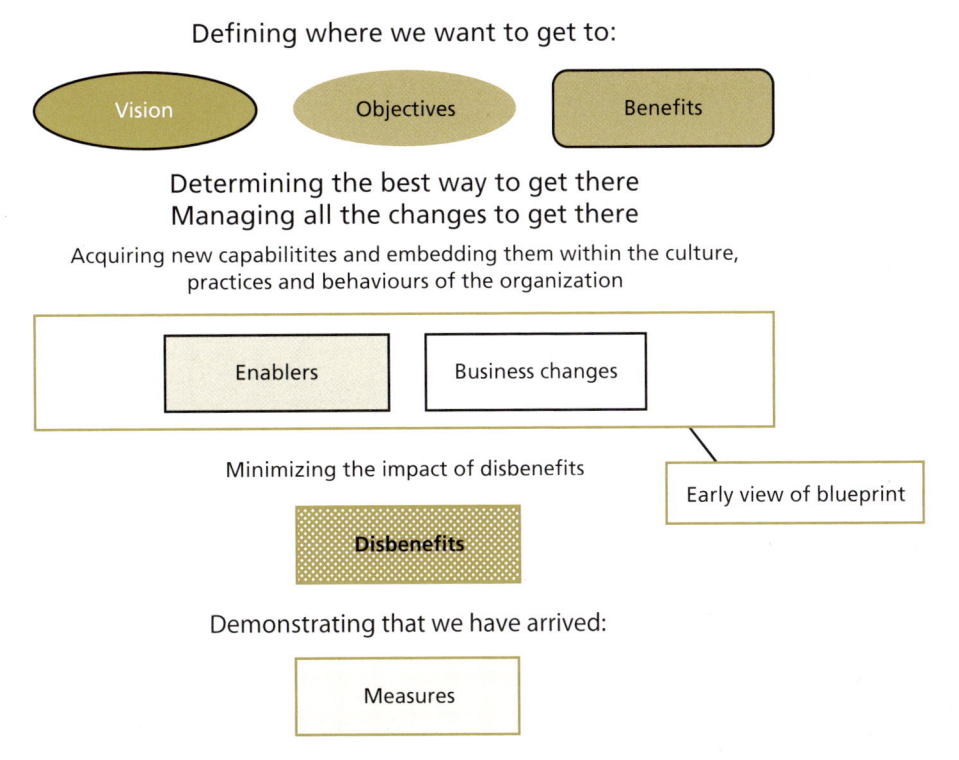

Measures

Figure 2.2 Framework for success

- Implementing the enablers and business changes in an optimum manner, including a benefit-focused sequence.
- Identifying and minimizing the impact of potential disbenefits.

Demonstrating that you have arrived involves:

- Determining a suitable set of measures
- Planning the capture of any additional metrics this may require
- Negotiating suitable targets and timescales for the benefits
- Regularly reporting progress against these measures, at least until the targets have been achieved.

This process for achieving success is described more fully in Chapter 3.

2.2 QUALITY COMMUNICATION

Another important requirement for effective benefit realization is quality communication. This requires:

- A precise definition of terminology – a common language
- Clear use of language when describing benefits and any of the other entities associated with benefit realization
- Extensive use of the visual – pictures, diagrams, charts, tables, colour etc. – particularly when describing relationships and dependencies.

Because good communication is so essential, section 10.1 includes precise definitions for each of the main entities associated with benefit realization, and for some entities (objective and benefit) provides a recommended word structure.

2.3 THE CENTRALITY OF BRM TO EFFECTIVE CHANGE

BRM is, in fact, central to effective change and should determine and drive most other programme and project activities, as illustrated in Figure 2.3.

Figure 2.3 highlights both the importance and the scope of BRM. It is not a simple add-on to programme and project management and should be the central theme of any change activity. MSP refers to it as a continual process running through the whole lifecycle of change.

Therefore, realizing benefits should not only be at the heart of change but should be recognized as a demanding and challenging activity in itself, and never be taken lightly. Such a critical activity needs to be:

- Planned and budgeted
- Underpinned by a proven process
- Resourced with skilled practitioners who have a track record of experience
- Backed by senior management, including the main board.

2.4 THE NEED FOR A STANDARD APPROACH

It is highly desirable to move as rapidly as possible to a single standard approach to BRM across an organization. If this is an industry-recognized process, such as the one described in this publication, this should help to achieve a common approach.

A standard approach to BRM will:

- Make best use of scarce BRM skills and increase the mobility of BRM staff
- Facilitate comparisons between different programmes and projects, enabling the

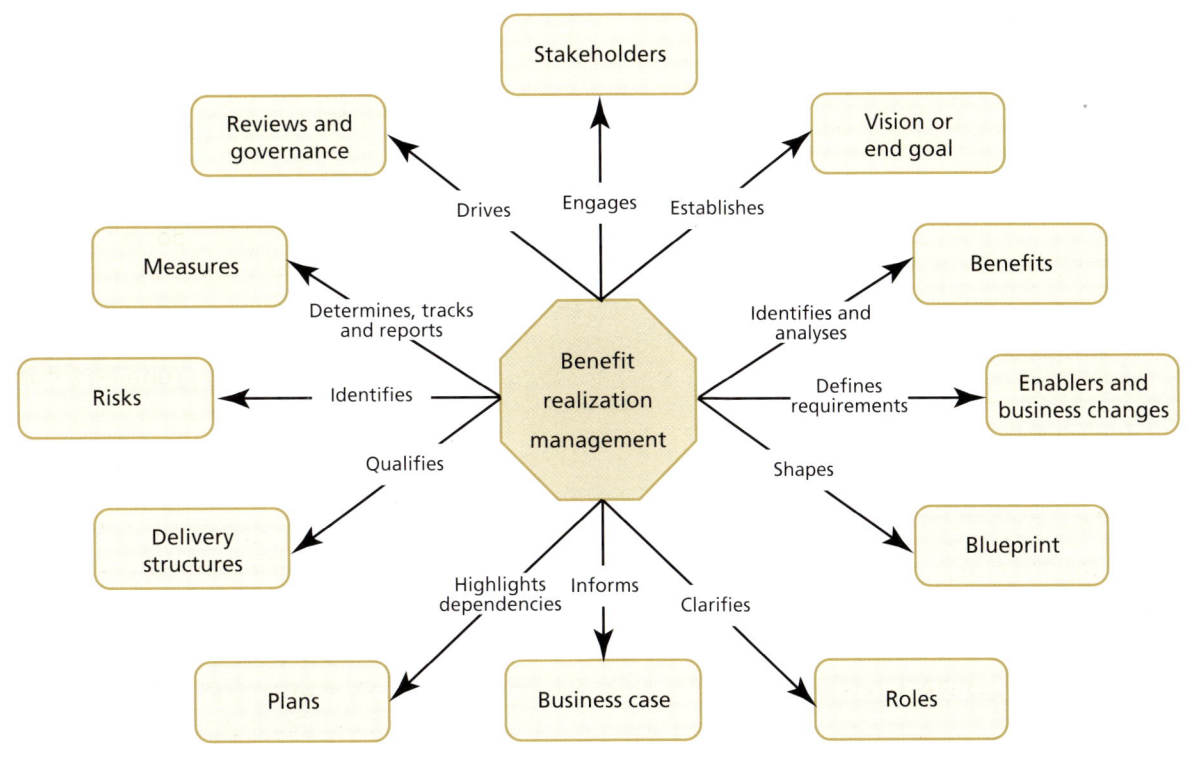

Requirements for effective benefit realization | 13

Figure 2.3 BRM – key driver for change

portfolio board to establish and maintain an effective and high-value portfolio
- Support any independent review processes, such as OGC's Gateway process.

Because BRM is scalable, within a single approach there could be a small number of different flavours to suit the different levels of scalability required for different types of change initiative. In particular, the approach for a programme is likely to differ from the approach for a project.

2.5 STAKEHOLDER ENGAGEMENT

Benefit realization will not be effective without appropriate stakeholder engagement. Both the OGC and the NAO cite lack of stakeholder engagement as one of the main reasons why programmes and projects fail.

It is often extremely challenging to secure sufficient engagement from busy business managers and staff, yet without their involvement many benefits are unlikely to be identified, owned or realized and the programme may be doomed to failure. For these reasons stakeholder engagement, often through workshops, is a key component of the BRM process.

2.6 THE IMPORTANCE OF NON-FINANCIAL BENEFITS

A financial benefit is one that directly involves real money – more money coming in to the organization or less money going out of the organization. With this definition most benefits arising from change are non-financial, but are nevertheless extremely important. They can still have baselines, targets and improvement timescales and should be monitored as part of the benefit tracking and reporting. The realization of a non-financial benefit is often a key step to achieving a subsequent financial benefit; so by ignoring the non-financial benefits the consequential financial benefits are unlikely to be realized.

There is a tendency to try to give financial values to non-financial benefits. This is dangerous because it:

- Distorts the truth and therefore misleads
- Can easily result in double counting
- Is tantamount to fraud if this pseudo-financial value is used as part of an investment justification.

In certain situations it may be appropriate to give a non-financial benefit an economic value for comparative purposes. However, this should not be confused with a real financial value. For a more detailed look at the importance of non-financial benefits see Chapter 10.

2.7 CRITICAL SUCCESS FACTORS FOR EFFECTIVE BENEFIT REALIZATION

In summary, the following are the top critical success factors for effective benefit realization:

- Putting the horse before the cart – starting with the end in view and then determining the solution (the required changes) and not vice versa
- Quality communication – using a common language and visuals
- Recognizing the centrality of BRM
- Adopting, as standard across the organization, a proven process for BRM
- Effective and continual engagement of stakeholders at all levels
- Giving due prominence to business change
- Giving due prominence to non-financial benefits.

3 The BRM process

3.1 PROCESS ESSENTIALS

As depicted in Figure 2.2, a successful BRM process involves:

- Defining where we want to get to
- Determining the best way to get there
- Managing all the changes to get there
- Demonstrating that we have arrived.

The process can be applied at any level within an organization and so is relevant to portfolio management, programme management and project management. We have successfully used, for many years, an expansion of these four steps into six practical phases, with a review point or gate between each phase (see Figure 3.1).

The change process model in Figure 6.1 of MSP is very similar to Figure 3.1 here except that it includes an initial phase clarifying the need for change. Generally, we would see this clarification as part of the 'set vision and objectives' phase.

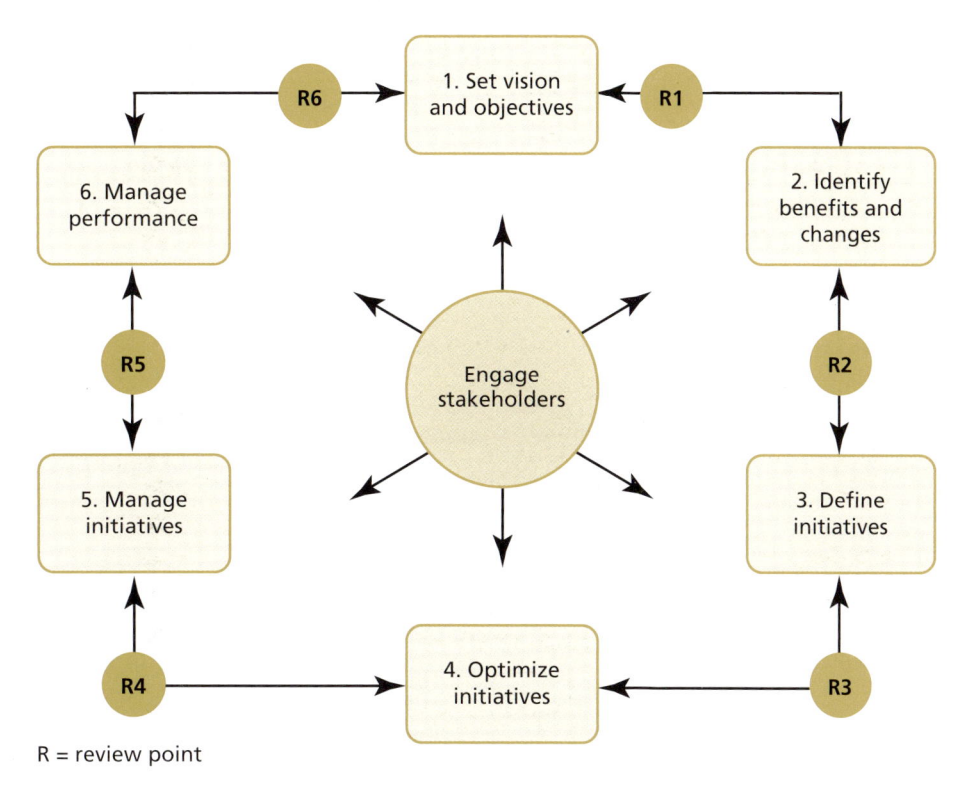

R = review point

Figure 3.1 The six phases of the change lifecycle

3.2 CHARACTERISTICS AND IMPLICATIONS OF THIS LIFECYCLE

The lifecycle is cyclical so that if, at the conclusion of the change, the vision and objectives have not been fully achieved, additional change activity may be triggered to plug the gap.

Although the main flow is clockwise, the arrows in Figure 3.1 go both ways indicating that iteration is encouraged, with a revisiting of earlier activities to refine expectations and plans in the light of better understanding and analysis or changes in the business environment. This is especially relevant where an organization, contrary to best practice, starts in Phase 3 with the creation of a programme.

A fundamental characteristic of the lifecycle is that stakeholders are engaged throughout the process, where a stakeholder is someone who can influence the change, positively or negatively, whether or not affected by it. This clearly includes anyone 'who can throw a spanner in the works' and anyone who is a victim of the change. In Phase 1 this engagement is usually with a few senior managers, representing key stakeholder groups. Movement through the lifecycle engages progressively larger numbers of stakeholders at lower levels in the organization.

Consideration of how stakeholders can best be engaged will be dealt with as the detailed activities of the lifecycle are explored in later chapters. MSP provides a more general but very helpful account of stakeholder engagement.

The ideal starting point for any change is Phase 1, set vision and objectives. This phase scopes the potential programme, clarifying the need for change and defining the end goal, by answering the questions:

- Why do we want or need to change?
- Where are we trying to get to?

Once a set of clear objectives has been determined and agreed by the senior stakeholders, and there is commitment to proceed to Phase 2, benefits can be identified which will underpin and ensure the delivery of the objectives. These benefits are best determined and related together using a mapping process. Once benefit maps have been refined and agreed, they can be used to determine the required enablers and business changes.

Although this requirement definition process will not immediately provide sufficient detail to build the enablers and manage the business change or issue invitations to tender (ITTs) or requests for proposals (RFPs), its value lies in:

- The business buy-in resulting from the stakeholder engagement process used to create the maps
- The way the many complex relationships between changes and benefits can be visually represented
- The speed with which diverse aspirations can be related, summarized and transformed into a feasible way forward.

If there is sufficient commitment to the benefits underpinning the objectives and to the enablers and changes required to deliver the benefits, the process can move to Phase 3 for more detailed work, including:

- The identification and merging of any duplicate benefits
- The identification of suitable measures for the benefits
- Determination of baselines, targets and timescales

- The identification and merging of duplicate enablers and business changes
- Checking to see if any of the required changes are being delivered by other programmes or projects
- Prioritizing and costing the new enablers and business changes
- Defining the initiatives needed to deliver the changes and determining a suitable programme and project structure
- Developing and securing agreement to the business case to proceed.

Once the business case has been approved, Phase 4 can begin. During Phase 4:

- Tenders can be accepted
- Enablers can be acquired or built
- The main change process can be started
- Benefit tracking and reporting can begin
- More detailed optimization can proceed.

Phase 5 involves the implementation of enablers and business changes in all the relevant business areas across, and often outside of, the organization.

Phase 6 pulls together all the results of benefit tracking and reporting, which may have started in Phase 3 but became fully established in Phase 4. These results are used to assess progress towards the fulfilment of the vision and achievement of the end objectives. Any shortfall may trigger remedial action or the creation of additional change activity to fill the gap. Reviews can be undertaken and lesson learned captured and disseminated.

In the ideal scenario, described above, the initiatives (programme and projects) are only defined in Phase 3 and formally established in Phase 3 or Phase 4, depending upon whether the full programme structure should be set up before the approval of the business case. However, the process is flexible enough to accommodate projects and programmes that are already underway when entry to the lifecycle would be in Phase 3. Some backtracking may then be required to fill any serious gaps in the identification and analysis of benefits.

Where the programmes and projects are only formally established in Phase 3, or even Phase 4, it is important to consider who is going to lead and facilitate the stakeholders through Phases 1 and 2. The most suitable person to do this is the benefit facilitator (or, in MSP, the benefit realization manager) because they:

- Are available before the programme or project manager has been identified and started
- Should have the necessary business understanding, good facilitation skills and expertise in BRM
- Are likely to assess and compare new ideas objectively and on a reasonably consistent basis.

The benefit facilitator would also be available after the programme and project teams have moved on to their next assignments. For more details of the benefit facilitator role see Chapter 11.

The generic six-phase lifecycle described in this chapter, and expanded in Part 2, fits well with most established programme and project management methodologies, such as MSP and PRINCE2™. This lifecycle can also be applied at portfolio level. Sometimes approaches need to be refined slightly to ensure that they can be properly integrated.

3.3 GATEWAYS AND REVIEWS

At the end of each of the six phases there should be a review to consider the case for proceeding through the gate to the next phase. These are internal reviews, where the review board for Phases 1, 2 and 6 is likely to be the portfolio board and, for Phases 3, 4 and 5, the programme or project board (although the portfolio board may also be involved in the business case review at the close of Phase 3).

The documents to be considered at these reviews are detailed in the phase descriptions in Chapters 4–9, and summarized in Chapter 14.

In a creative environment where lots of ideas for change are generated, it is likely that many of these would be rejected or deferred at the close of Phase 1, a smaller number at the close of Phase 2 and only rarely at the close of Phase 3 or later.

In addition to these internal reviews it is often helpful to undertake, at key stages, external reviews such as an OGC Gateway review.

3.4 FLEXIBILITY AND VALUE OF THE PROCESS

Because it is cyclical, the process is flexible and can be entered at any stage and therefore applied to existing programmes and projects. It is also iterative and so can accommodate reworking any phase or part phase; and adjustments to analysis, plans and documents can be made in the light of later experience. The process is particularly applicable to programmes as these are often moulded and refined through their lifecycle.

BRM is valuable because:

- It is a powerful tool for scoping change, often leading to reductions in planned costs
- The process engages stakeholders throughout, securing commitment to the change and the initiative's ultimate success
- Non-financial benefits are taken seriously and, as a result, more financial benefits are delivered, as they are usually the consequence of several intermediate non-financial benefits
- The process frequently brings forward in time the realization of financial benefits and sustains them for longer
- Overall, it is likely to increase significantly the realization of benefits from change, sometimes from 20% to 80% of potential benefits.

Part 2
Applying BRM to programmes and projects

4 Applying BRM Phase 1: set vision and objectives

4.1 THE STARTING POINT

The following chapters will each consider, in turn, the six phases of the BRM process introduced in Chapter 3, with particular reference to programmes and projects. Although the approach can be applied to both programmes and projects, to avoid complexity in the text, the target change initiative is taken as a programme containing several projects.

Although the process is cyclical and can be started in any phase, the greatest value will be generated by starting with Phase 1.

When applying BRM to a new initiative, it is worth briefly considering the likely existing environment:

- There will be an existing portfolio of change initiatives – programmes and projects
- There will hopefully be a portfolio board (perhaps called something different), which sanctions new projects and oversees the whole portfolio
- The idea for the new initiative may have come top-down or bottom-up, and may be expressed as a vision, a new business state or just an idea for change
- The potential new idea has backing from at least one business manager in order to justify the exploratory effort required for Phase 1.

The first step in considering a new idea is to identify the main stakeholders and engage them. The recommended method of engagement is through a well-facilitated workshop.

4.2 WORKSHOP TO DEFINE AND MAP OBJECTIVES

Phase 1 is likely to require a single half-day workshop with senior representatives from the key stakeholders.

Managers often have different views about why a particular change is being introduced, and this may be true even when there is already an established programme and a documented business case. This diversity is usually indicative of one or more of the following:

- Managers have different backgrounds and aspirations
- Business cases are only seen as a justification and not as a description of the end goal and required direction
- There are too many objectives to assimilate easily
- Some so-called objectives are answering the 'how' question and not the 'why' question
- Objectives, even if understood, are not owned by the whole management team.

To address these issues and to establish the scope of the change initiative, the following workshop process is recommended. Using this approach and provided there is good representative stakeholder participation, the workshop should enable the determination, refinement and agreement of a set of genuine objectives, which are owned by the whole management team.

The process starts with an open question relating to the broad scope or vision, if already defined – for example: 'Why do we want to improve document handling?' It is always a 'why' question and it should not imply or even hint at a solution. Therefore, 'Why do we want a new document management system?' would not be an appropriate question to ask.

If it is likely that some workshop participants feel that there is no need for change, the facilitator should arm themselves with evidence to contest this view – for example, if the likely question is: 'Why do we need to improve customer service?' then evidence of customer complaints, lost sales and bad press should be available. This could be discussed in the first part of the workshop or distributed beforehand as part of any pre-workshop briefing.

Workshop participants are asked to write four or five short answers to the chosen 'why' question. The cards are then clustered around common themes on a large display board and a summary card is written for each cluster. Summary cards are written as improvement objectives, where an objective is an answer to the 'why' question and defines purpose, direction and aim. It is recommended that each objective is written beginning with the word 'to'. Blue cards are normally used for objectives. (For further detail on these conventions see Chapter 10.)

This process typically results in 10–15 (and occasionally up to 20) objectives. For practical reasons, both within the programme and for wider stakeholder communication, it is extremely important to focus on a much smaller set, usually between two and four objectives. The next step is to identify the most appropriate reduced set of objectives.

It could be tempting to utilize the experience of the senior stakeholders and ask them to vote on the shortlist of objectives. This would be a sensible process if all the original objectives were independent of each other, but this is rarely the case.

The objective cards are then placed on a new board in a cause-and-effect relationship diagram, referred to as a strategy map (see Figure 4.1), with the ultimate goal on the right-hand side.

The strategy map in Figure 4.1 was developed with a senior management team from one of the high-street banks, and relates to a proposed change initiative to embed BRM throughout the bank.

Creating high-quality robust maps is not a trivial exercise and requires skill and experience. As a result, Chapter 12 is dedicated to mapping.

To move from the initial ten objectives, illustrated in Figure 4.1, to a set of two, three or four 'bounding' objectives, it's important to consider the responsibilities of two key people – the programme manager and the person providing the funding, the sponsor.

Considering the far right objective in Figure 4.1, 'To increase shareholder value', it would clearly be inappropriate to hold the programme manager accountable for achieving this, so it sits beyond the scope of the programme. Similarly, the sponsor would consider the objective 'To increase understanding of BRM' totally inadequate as an ultimate objective and would not sanction funding just to achieve this.

If we now continue the assessment, working through all the objectives in Figure 4.1 from right to left and applying the same kind of considerations, we fairly quickly arrive at the following three objectives, to bound the scope and summarize the purpose of the programme:

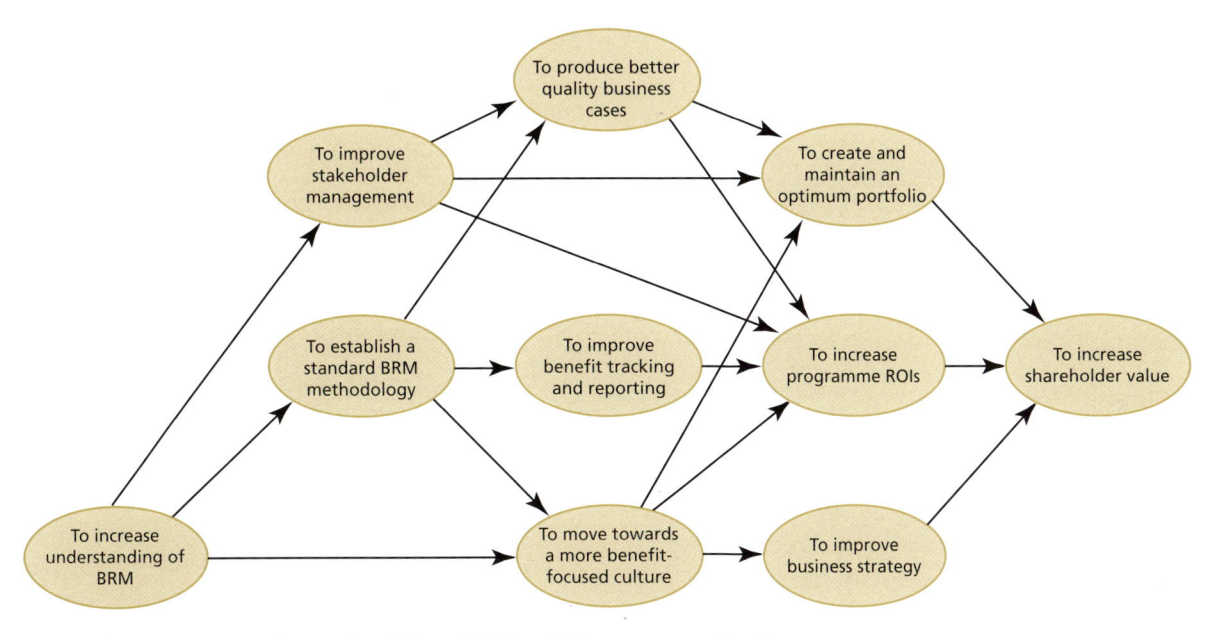

Applying BRM Phase 1: set vision and objectives | 23

Figure 4.1 Strategy map for embedding BRM within an organization

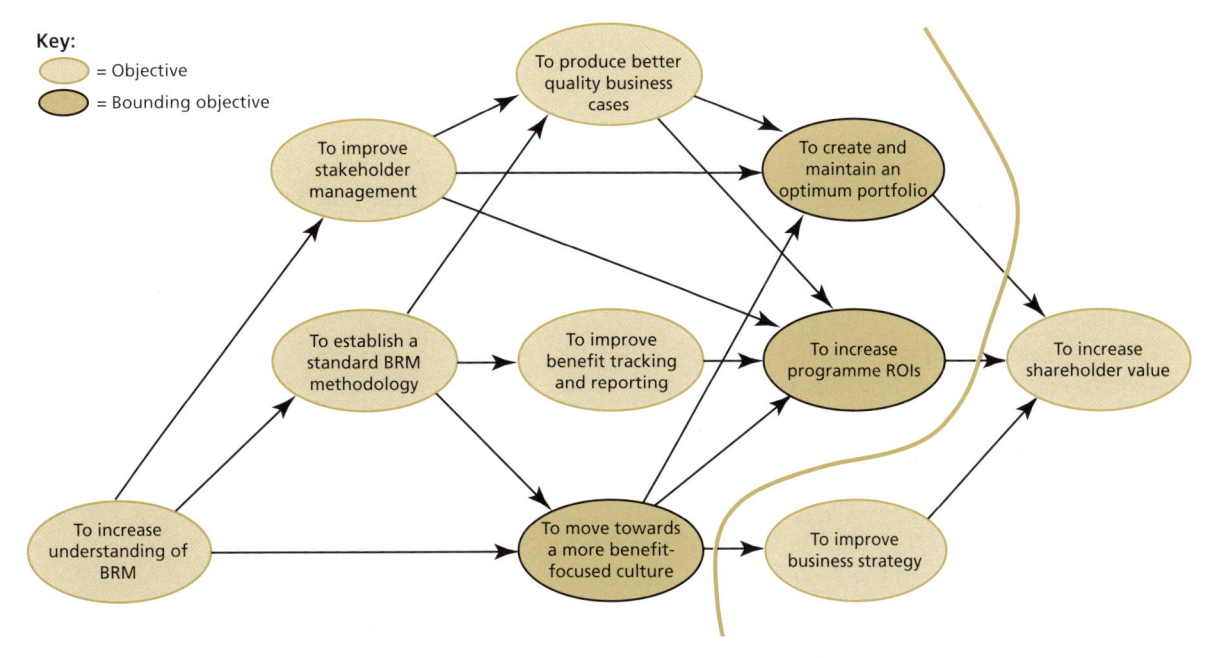

Figure 4.2 Strategy map with bounding objectives and programme boundary

- To create and maintain an optimum portfolio
- To increase programme ROIs
- To move towards a more benefit-focused culture.

These are the farthest to the right that the programme manager would countenance, in terms of accountability for achievement, and they are sufficiently far to the right for the sponsor to be prepared to fund them. Figure 4.2 highlights the bounding objectives and programme boundary.

Ideally the three bounding objectives highlighted in Figure 4.2 would be mutually independent and therefore appear below one another in the diagram. However, this is not often possible.

If there is difficulty in agreeing a set of bounding objectives, it may be helpful to first weight the paths in at least the right-hand part of Figure 4.1 (see sections 6.3 and 12.3).

The whole process should be facilitated and the management team brought in at every stage.

Although the primary purpose for creating the strategy map is the determination of, and agreement to, the bounding objectives, the map should not be discarded once these objectives have been determined. It continues to represent a valid path to the achievement of these objectives, and the consequential impact they may have. The map would be valuable to the programme team and it can form a useful attachment to a business case. It would also be of interest to the portfolio board, with its responsibility for actively managing the whole portfolio.

The bounding objectives will normally contribute to one or more end objectives and/or a vision whose total fulfilment is beyond the responsibility of the programme manager, but which nevertheless describes the ultimate reason for undertaking the programme. Figure 4.3 links the bounding objectives to a vision.

In addition to agreeing the bounding objectives, the workshop participants need to be committed to their achievement and supportive of the continuing exploration of the potential programme.

4.3 FURTHER ANALYSIS AND DOCUMENTATION

Further checks, undertaken outside the workshop, should include:

- How the bounding objectives contribute to the organization's strategy and objectives – alignment
- How this potential programme fits with the existing portfolio – balance.

Alignment may already be indicated by the strategy map – for example, where the bounding objectives contribute directly to one or more of the organization's objectives. Alignment may also be defined using a matrix (see Figure 4.4).

When assessing alignment, it is insufficient to state that there is alignment, some indication of contribution is required, or that the minimum indication should be high, medium or low contribution. In some situations it should be possible to give the percentage contribution to some of the organization's targets.

In considering how the potential programme would fit with the rest of the existing portfolio a number of factors should be investigated, including:

- Portfolio balance
- Impact on stakeholders
- Resource requirements.

Applying BRM Phase 1: set vision and objectives | 25

Key:
- = Objective
- = Bounding objective
- = Vision

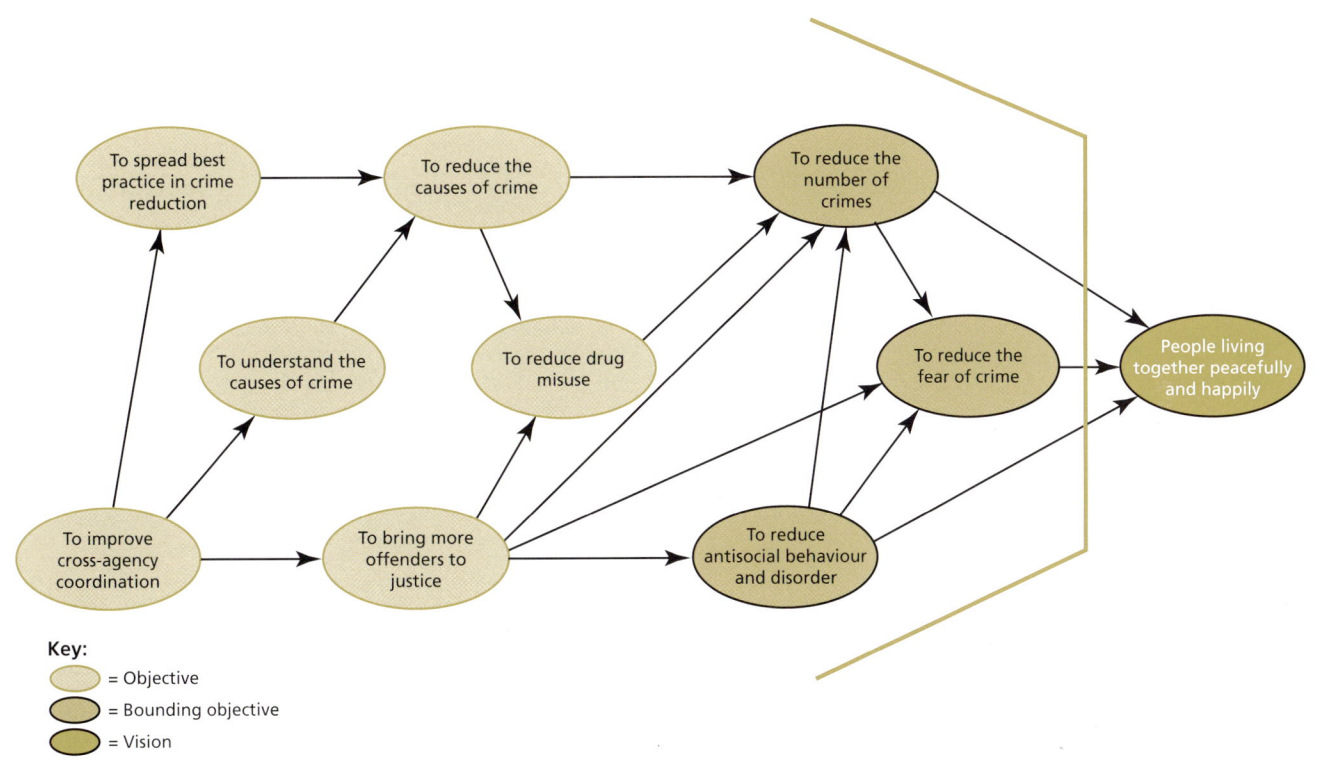

Figure 4.3 Linking objectives to a vision

Business objective \ Programme objective	To create and maintain an optimum portfolio	To improve the ROI of programmes (and projects)	To move towards a more benefit-focused culture
To develop and grow the business	High impact	Medium impact	High impact
To improve service to customers	Medium impact	High impact	Medium impact
To increase profitability	Medium impact	High impact	High impact
To develop staff towards greater agility and openness to change	Low impact	Low impact	High impact

Figure 4.4 Alignment of programme and business objectives

Strategic	Speculative
Programmes which primarily support **future business opportunities** – e.g. business development, growth.	Programmes with a **high achievement risk**, but often high reward – e.g. arising from experimenting with the way we do things.
Programmes which will deliver **critical improvements to today's operations** – e.g. increased efficiency and effectiveness.	'Nice to have' programmes, in the sense that the organization's growth or survival will not depend on them. Usually related to improvements to non-critical activities. **Often quick wins.**
Key operational	**Support**

Figure 4.5 Programme categorization by business impact (the Cranfield Grid)

A very useful technique for looking at portfolio balance is the Cranfield Grid, developed by Cranfield University from the Boston Matrix and used to assess and balance a portfolio of programmes or projects. Programmes and projects are classified according to the four cells in the grid (see Figure 4.5).

The programme under consideration would need to be classified using the matrix illustrated in Figure 4.5, and then the impact of its inclusion in the portfolio assessed. This assessment would be related to the balance, in percentage terms, between the four quadrants, already determined for the particular organization by the portfolio board (see section 11.2 and Chapter 15).

Other relevant information includes:

- Scope – in terms of geography or function
- Timescale – indication of any critical deadlines.

The results from the workshop and subsequent analysis could be gathered together in a 'case for change' (effectively the programme mandate), which would then be the basis of the review to consider whether the investigation should proceed to Phase 2.

The content of the case for change might include:

- A vision statement
- **A strategy map of objectives with bounding objectives highlighted**
- **Context or strategic fit – demonstration of alignment with the organization's mission and objectives**
- **Scope – boundaries within which the programme will work**
- **Time constraints – critical deadlines or windows of opportunity**
- **Stakeholders engaged, with an indication of their level of commitment**
- Anticipated improvements, which are expected as a result of the programme
- Solution ideas and delivery approaches.
- Any existing initiatives likely to be incorporated in this new initiative
- Dependencies.

The items in bold would usually be mandatory, and the rest optional.

Because this phase is an initial exploration of an idea for change there will not normally be a programme manager or a programme board. Therefore, it is recommended that the workshop and subsequent analysis is undertaken by the benefit facilitator and the concluding review by the portfolio board (see Chapter 11 for an explanation of these roles).

If the recommendation is to proceed to Phase 2 the strategy for applying BRM (referred to in MSP as the benefits management strategy) should be defined. If the organization has an established approach for BRM, this strategy should indicate how the standard approach is to be applied, including:

- The degree of scalability that is appropriate
- A description of the function, roles and responsibilities for benefit planning and realization (if this is not already part of the organization's documented approach to BRM)
- **The names of the individuals nominated to fill these roles**
- **The plan for applying BRM to the programme, including stakeholders to be engaged, intended workshops etc.**
- Measurement methods and processes to be used to monitor and assess the realization of benefits.

If there is an established approach for BRM to which the strategy refers, it should be no more than one page as a single document, or a section within the programme mandate.

Within this phase an issues log should be set up to register issues which, if not addressed, could become risks, and a risk register to capture and actively manage the risks. The risk register should include the risks:

- To the organization (or parts of it) from undertaking the change
- Of not realizing the benefits
- Arising from potential disbenefits.

For each risk, the risk register should include:

- A description of the risk
- The probability of the risk occurring
- The impact on the programme should the risk materialize
- The likely timescale for the risk materializing
- A description of the proposed action to mitigate the risk
- The actionee – the individual assigned to take the above action
- Changed values of any of the above as a consequence of the action.

The effort required to undertake this phase is likely to be:

- About two days for the benefit facilitator
- Half a day for each of the senior stakeholder representatives
- About 15 minutes for the portfolio board.

5 Applying BRM Phase 2: identify benefits and changes

5.1 PHASE OVERVIEW

Once the bounding objectives have been identified and agreed, and the case for change (programme mandate) approved, the more detailed planning can proceed. Engaging and involving stakeholders will again be critical and, in this phase, they will usually be the next levels of management plus relevant technical experts. Again, workshops provide the ideal forum for stakeholder engagement and information gathering.

This phase involves:

- Confirming, analysing and grouping the stakeholders
- Identifying a comprehensive set of benefits and creating a benefits map for each bounding objective
- Developing a benefits distribution matrix for the programme
- Working on each benefits map to determine the required enablers and business changes
- Identifying and consolidating duplicate entities – benefits, enablers and business changes
- Identifying measures for the benefits
- Documenting the results for presentation to the review board.

5.2 ANALYSING AND ENGAGING STAKEHOLDERS

An initial assessment was undertaken early in Phase 1 and hopefully senior representatives of the main stakeholders participated in the phase workshop. Now with a clearer understanding of the scope of the potential programme, it is worth reconsidering the stakeholders identified. This can be done in two parts – initially at the start of the phase to determine who to engage in the phase workshops and then reviewed in the workshops to check that no important stakeholder has been missed.

Stakeholder engagement is a continual process running throughout the change lifecycle and it takes many forms. A powerful engagement forum is the workshop, which is also a very effective way of gathering the information needed to manage the programme and realize the benefits. Therefore, when planning workshops, it is important to seek the best mix of participants. The mix of invitees should:

- Cover the breadth of expertise relevant to the scope of workshop – whole programme or just a subset of the bounding objectives
- Include those who think strategically and creatively
- Include key influencers
- Include any vocal opponents to the programme.

Because there will be a large number of stakeholders for most programmes, it is helpful to cluster them in manageable groups. The criteria for clustering are:

Applying BRM Phase 2: identify benefits and changes | 29

- Will they receive similar benefits?
- Will they experience similar disbenefits?
- Will they be impacted by similar kinds of change?

Mind maps can be useful to represent the groups (see Figure 5.1).

5.3 BENEFIT IDENTIFICATION AND MAPPING

To identify a comprehensive set of potential benefits it is important to engage with the right stakeholders, ideally in one or more workshops. In this environment two or three different techniques can be applied separately to each objective:

- Open brainstorming to identify benefits which relate to the specific bounding objective, while considering the full range of stakeholders
- Using a framework, such as the Cranfield Grid, to identify benefits by type of impact
- Constructing a benefits map.

When applying these techniques it is important to understand what a benefit is and how it is best described. It is an outcome of change provided it is perceived as positive by the relevant stakeholders, and, ideally, should be measurable. Because it is an outcome of change, implying a before and after situation, it improves clarity if all benefits are described starting with an adjective indicating the direction of improvement – words

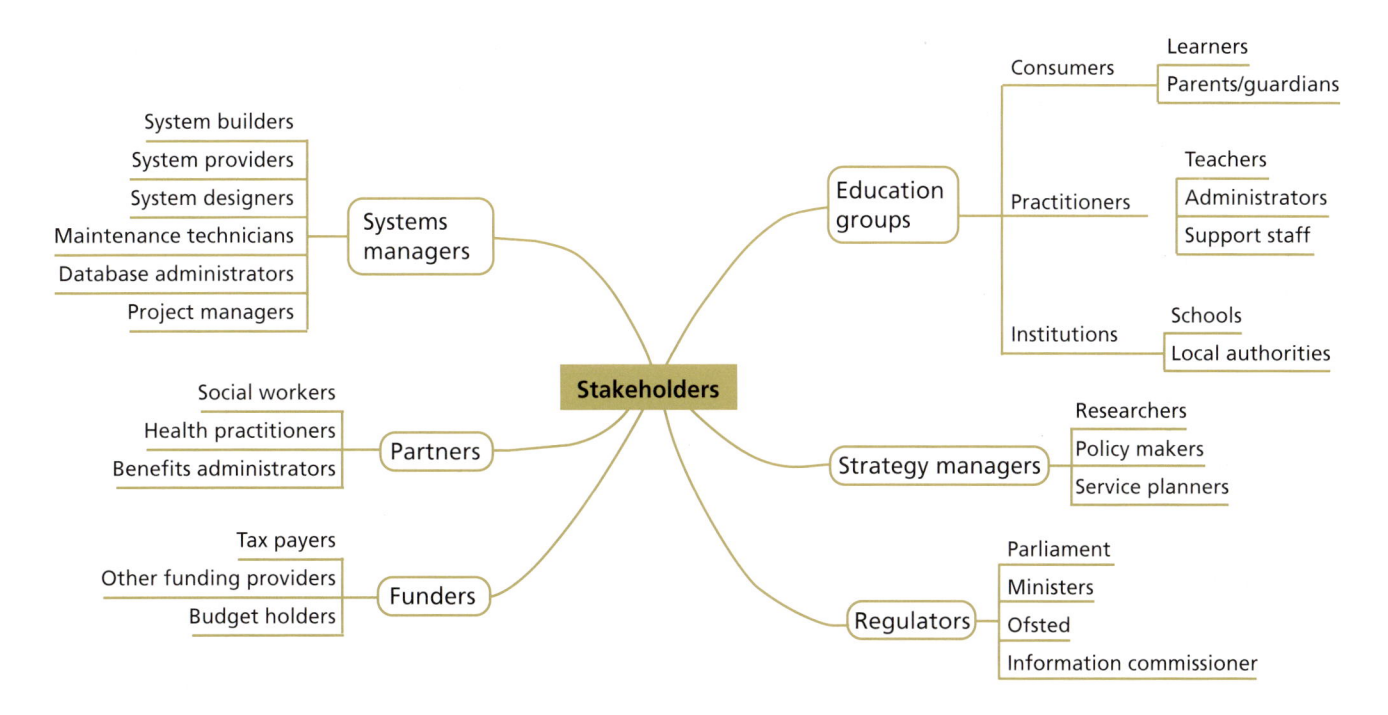

Figure 5.1 Representation of stakeholders and their grouping hierarchy

Part 2: Applying BRM to programmes and projects

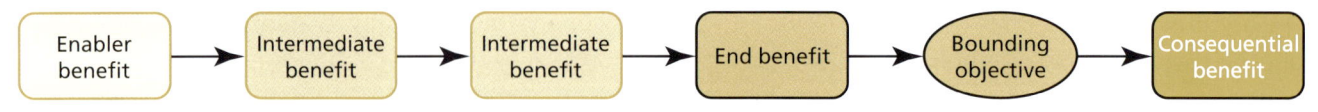

Figure 5.2 The relationship between different types of benefit

Enabler benefit → Intermediate benefit → Intermediate benefit → End benefit → Bounding objective → Consequential benefit

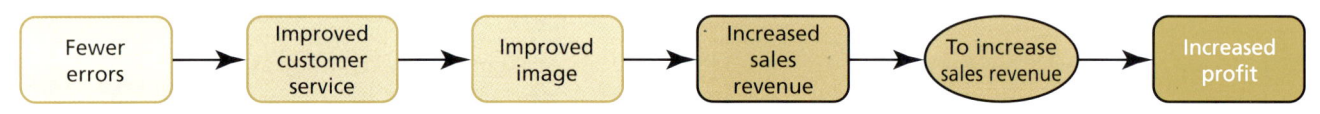

Figure 5.3 Examples of different types of benefit

Fewer errors → Improved customer service → Improved image → Increased sales revenue → To increase sales revenue → Increased profit

such as *improved*, *increased*, *fewer*, *more*, *faster*, *reduced*. A disbenefit is an outcome of change which is perceived as negative.

When capturing benefit suggestions it is helpful to use cards, as these can easily be moved around on boards, for grouping and for the creation of maps.

- Write all benefits (normally on green cards) using the language for benefits – that is, starting with an adjective indicating the anticipated direction of improvement (see Chapter 10 for more information on the definition, wording and classification of benefits). Write each benefit on a separate card.
- If disbenefits arise when considering benefits, capture these on red cards.
- Don't lose good ideas by not writing thoughts on cards. At this stage we want to encourage innovative thinking and not filter out any creative ideas – this can be done later if necessary. If we fail to capture a great idea it may be lost forever.

Identified benefits will tend to fall into one of four categories (see Figure 5.2).

Enabler benefits are those that will occur as a direct consequence of implementing an enabler and perhaps some related business change. End benefits are directly equivalent to the objective but in benefit language – usually more than one is required to achieve this equivalence (see Figure 5.4). Intermediate benefits lie between the enabler and end benefits and represent different kinds of improvement on the benefit journey. Consequential benefits are a consequence of having achieved the objective. Figure 5.3 shows examples of different types of benefit.

When applying the first technique it is quite usual to identify a wide mix of benefits, including several consequential benefits. Although we are primarily interested in those benefits that will ultimately deliver the objective, and so help to determine the requirements, the consequential benefits should not be discarded. They are likely to be of interest to the portfolio board and may be needed to create the justification part of the business case.

The second technique uses a framework based on the Cranfield Grid but applied to benefits rather than programmes (see Figure 4.5). Brainstorming, again, considers benefits related to the specific objective but potential business impact should also be taken into account.

The third technique focuses on constructing a benefits map, utilizing any benefits already identified by either of the previous techniques.

Applying BRM Phase 2: identify benefits and changes | **31**

Starting from this pool of benefits, but adding new ones as required, a set of end benefits must be determined which together are equivalent, in benefit speak, to the specific objective. This equivalence requires that the end benefits are:

- Collectively sufficient
- Individually necessary
- Mutually independent.

With this equivalence it is not necessary to measure, track and report the fulfilment of the objective but just the realization of the benefits.

Figure 5.4 shows three examples of bounding objectives, each with its own set of end benefits. In these three examples the end benefits were considered to be collectively sufficient to deliver the related objective, individually necessary and mutually independent. Those with two end benefits both have a numeric relationship with the objective, the first through summation and the second through multiplication. In the third example the end benefits are loosely related through process, where the process runs vertically down.

Additive

- Fewer crimes by re-offenders
- Fewer crimes by first-time criminals

→ To reduce the number of crimes

Multiplicative

- Increased throughput per session
- More sessions run

→ To improve the utilization of the hospital's operating theatres

End benefits based on process

- Better understanding of recruitment needs
- Improved sourcing of applicants
- Improved selection from the applicant pool
- Increased offer-acceptance rates
- Improved integration of new recruits

→ To improve recruitment

Key:
▢ = End benefit
⬭ = Bounding objective

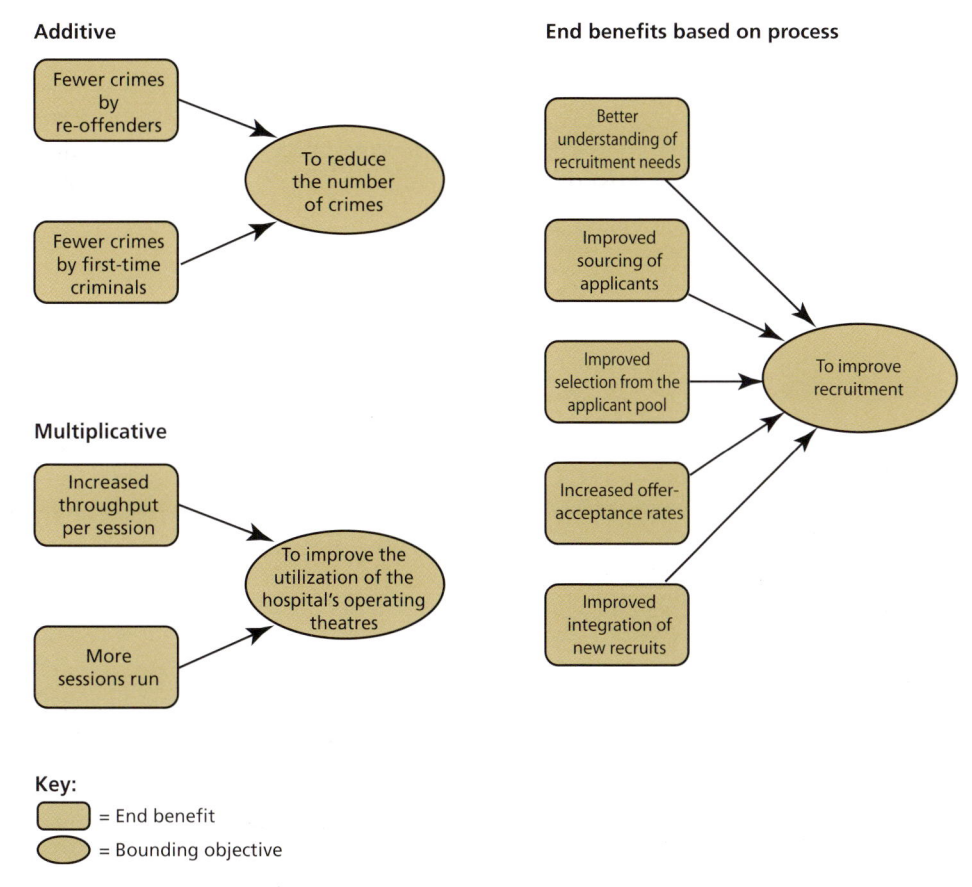

Figure 5.4 End benefits for different objectives

32 | Part 2: Applying BRM to programmes and projects

Key:
- ▭ = Intermediate benefit
- ▭ = End benefit
- ⬭ = Bounding objective
- ▦ = Disbenefit

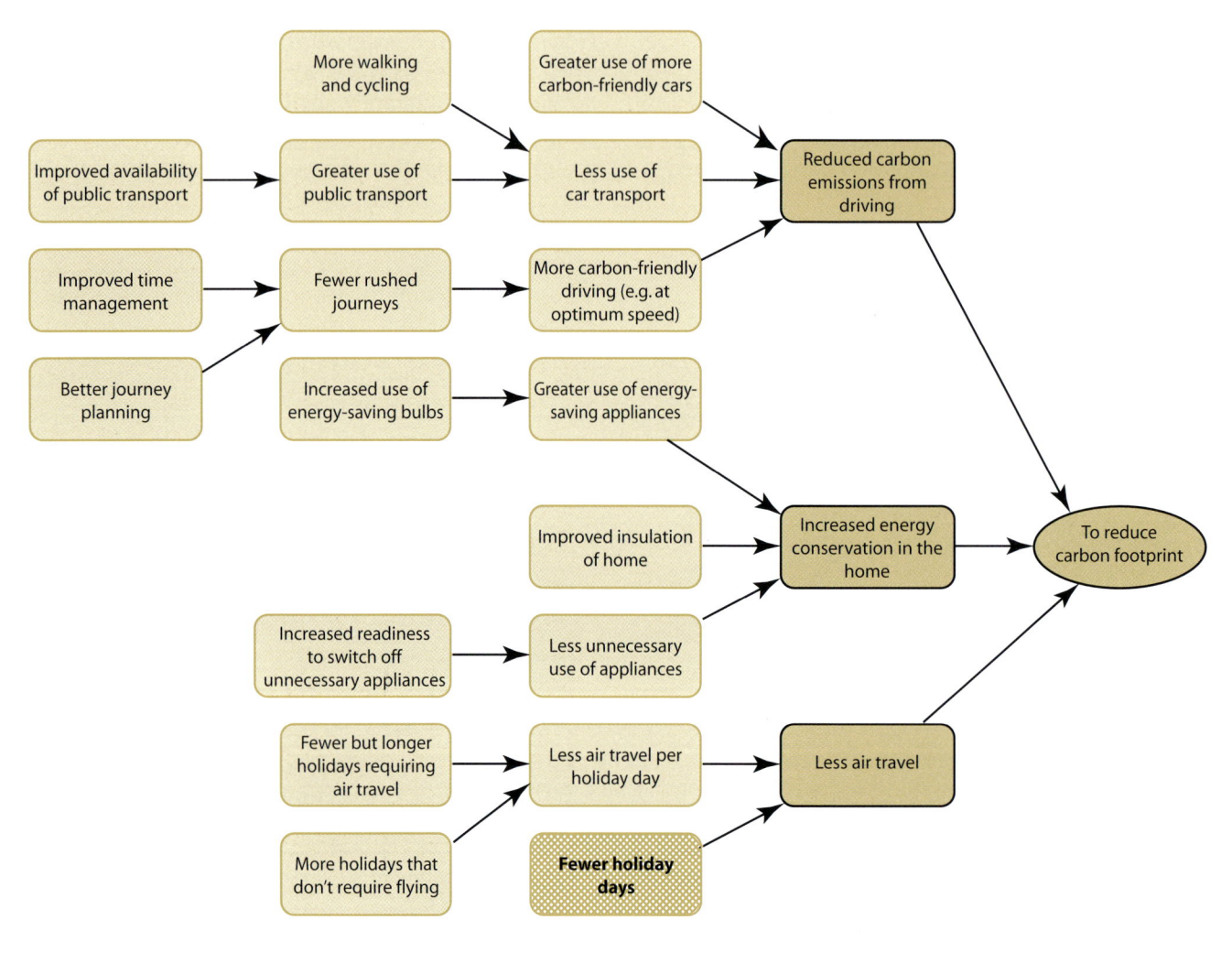

Figure 5.5 Example benefits map for reducing a carbon footprint

It should be noted that the lines linking entities in all BRM maps are based on cause and effect and not process. It is important to understand this distinction.

Once a set of end benefits is proposed, where realizing all of them would fully deliver the objective, each should be tested with the following questions:

- Does it directly contribute to any of the other end benefits?
- Does it contribute to any other benefit which itself contributes to an end benefit?
- If it is removed from the set would achievement of the remainder still fully deliver the objective?

If the answer to any of these questions is 'Yes' then it is not an end benefit.

Once there is confidence in the set of end benefits the intermediate benefits contributing to the end benefits can be determined. This process continues working right to left until the benefits map is complete. Since the whole map is built working from the end benefits, it is worth ensuring that they are robust and the foundation is solid. An example of a benefits map developed for someone who wants to reduce their carbon footprint is given in Figure 5.5.

This is effectively a systematic decomposition working right to left using the criteria of individual necessity and mutual independence. The third criterion of 'collective sufficiency' is progressively relaxed during the movement to the left. Mapping is explained in greater detail in Chapter 12.

5.4 DEVELOPING A BENEFIT DISTRIBUTION MATRIX

For all three of the identification processes described in section 5.3 (brainstorm, framework and benefits map), every time a card is written it should be marked with code letters indicating the stakeholder group(s) that will experience either the benefit or the disbenefit. This will enable the subsequent production of a benefit distribution matrix for the programme, as illustrated in Figure 5.6.

The matrix in Figure 5.6 highlights those stakeholders who are likely to receive more disbenefits than benefits, and so not be motivated to cooperate with the implementation of the required changes. By recognizing this problem at a relatively early stage, it may be possible to slightly change the original scope (for a small incremental cost), to deliver more benefits to the demotivated stakeholders.

Even where this is not feasible, it is still valuable to understand where demotivation may exist in order to give greater attention to these stakeholders, and in particular to:

- Explore how disbenefits may be minimized
- Communicate the big picture, especially the wider spread of benefits
- Communicate what is in it for the customers.

5.5 REQUIREMENTS DEFINITION

When first created, the benefits map is nothing more than a wish list – but not a random wish list. It has been carefully constructed working from an agreed bounding objective, using just logic and a good understanding of the business environment. Other considerations, such as feasibility, resource requirements and costs are handled later in the process.

The next step is to start to identify the changes necessary to deliver the benefits. This process starts on the left-hand side of the map; each benefit is considered in turn and the changes required to deliver the benefit are determined – these changes are normally a combination of enablers

Key benefits and disbenefits by stakeholder	Board	Sponsor (e.g. SRO) and programme board	Programme director/manager	Business change manager	Programme team	Enabler project teams	Business manager	Business user
Benefit								
More optimum programme portfolio	■	■					■	
Earlier recognition of ineffective programmes	■	■						
Improved stakeholder engagement			■	■	■		■	■
Clearer sense of direction			■	■	■		■	■
More effective programme management			■	■	■			
Better use of resources			■	■				
Improved management of risk			■	■				
Reduced enabler costs		■	■	■	■			
More financial benefits realized	■	■	■	■				
More non-financial benefits realized			■	■			■	■
Greater visibility of realized benefits		■	■	■				
Improved programme image			■	■				
Disbenefit								
Extra effort by the business							▨	▨
Slower start to the programme						▨	▨	▨
Enabler project targets threatened						▨		

Figure 5.6 Benefits and disbenefits of BRM by stakeholder

Applying BRM Phase 2: identify benefits and changes | 35

and business changes. Adding all the identified enablers and business changes to the benefits map transforms it into a benefit dependency map (BDM).

If there are three bounding objectives there are likely to be three BDMs. This set of dependency maps will represent a good description of the target business state and constitutes a high-level picture of the blueprint. This view of the blueprint has been built around the bounding objectives. Other views will also be important – for example, views structured around business function – in order to gain a comprehensive picture.

Although this process will not immediately create the detail required to build systems or issue ITTs or RFPs, it is nevertheless a powerful requirements definition process, since it identifies the necessary business changes in addition to the enabler features, and relates both to potential benefits.

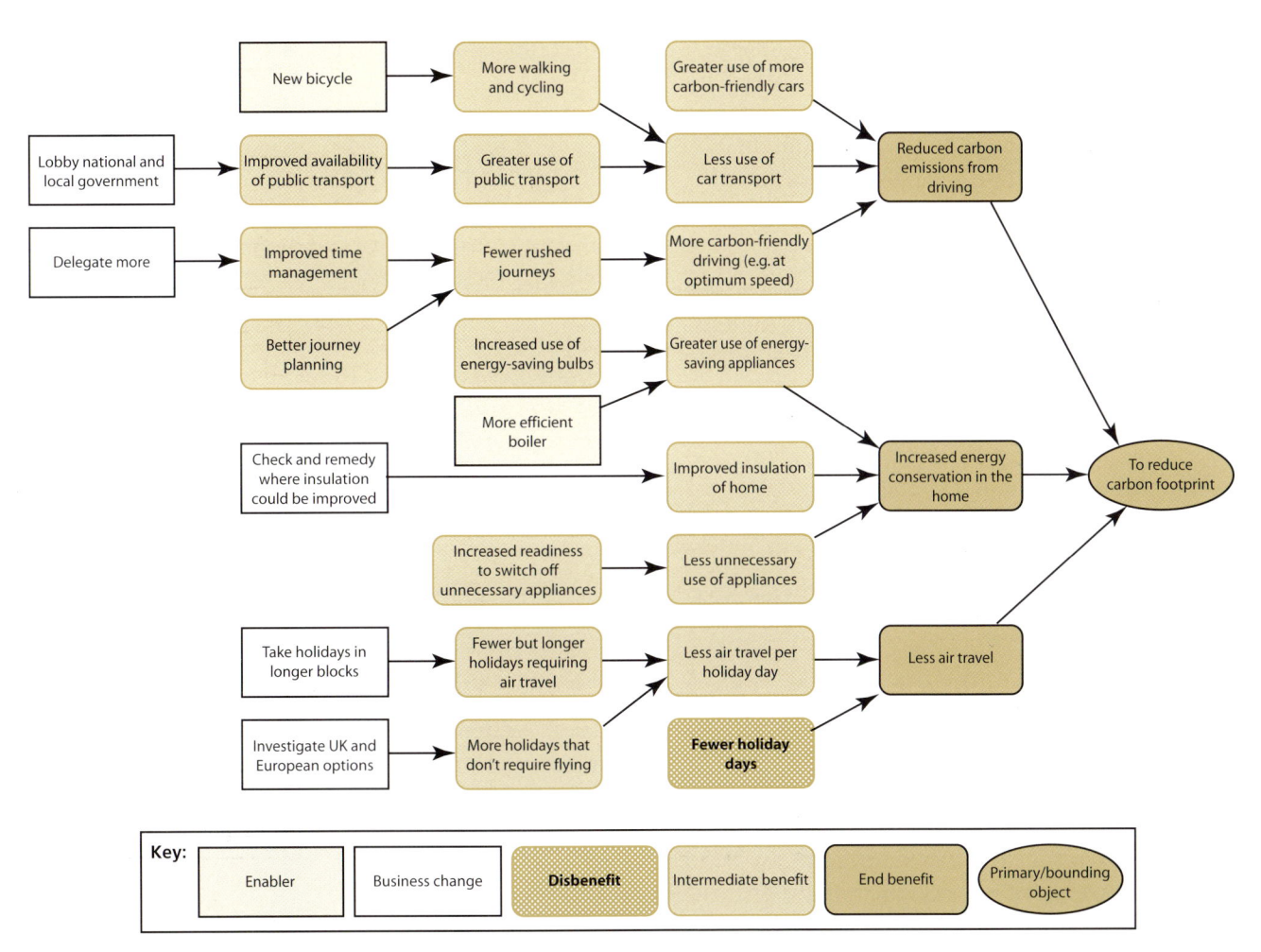

Figure 5.7 Example BDM for reducing a carbon footprint

A simple example of a partially developed BDM for the benefits map in Figure 5.5 is illustrated in Figure 5.7.

Creating good quality maps requires experience, skill and the right aptitude. Further examples, including tips for constructing a BDM, are given in Chapter 12.

5.6 IDENTIFYING AND CONSOLIDATING DUPLICATE ENTITIES

Generally, a programme will have only three or four BDMs, although for major transformation programmes there could be as many as 12. Having multiple BDMs usually means that there will be a duplication of benefits, enablers and business changes. These will need to be identified and consolidated.

If there are only two or three maps it is best to use the maps to search for potential duplicate benefits. With four or more maps, list the benefits and then group them using one of the classifications suggested in section 10.2. This is only likely to occur when there are four or more bounding objectives – this should rarely happen and is generally not recommended.

Once potential duplicate benefits are identified further checks are needed to be sure the benefits are the same, including:

- Do they have the same stakeholders as beneficiaries?
- Are they the consequence of the same or similar changes?

Identical benefits need to be consolidated with a common description and applied to all maps. With suitable software this is a straightforward process.

With enablers and business changes it is important not only to identify exact duplication but also to recognize similarity and synergy – for example, if one map needs a skills database, another needs a staff availability database; these requirements could be combined in a single enabler.

Following the consolidation of duplicate or similar requirements it will be important to check whether these are planned for delivery by other projects or programmes. This could be undertaken in this phase or the next, which is where it is more fully described.

5.7 IDENTIFYING MEASURES FOR THE BENEFITS

Once benefit consolidation is complete measures should be identified for the benefits. This is best done in a separate smaller workshop when participants are fresh and alert. In this instance the workshop participants should include the likely benefit owners so that they can approve the measures and help determine and subsequently own the benefit targets.

As a starting point, look for at least one measure for every benefit. If some benefits are particularly hard to measure you could settle for measuring the benefits either side of the difficult ones. This works best where there is only a single link into and out of the difficult benefit and the achievement timescales are not too far apart.

In most organizations there will be resistance to measuring all the benefits in a benefits map. Objections may include:

- It is unnecessary
- It would be too time-consuming and costly

- We don't have the resource
- Surely we only need to measure the key benefits.

This is such an important subject that it is essential to carefully consider these objections. Remember that a map is a set of cause-and-effect relationships, so the benefits on the right-hand side will only be achieved once the feeder benefits have been realized. If only the right-hand benefits are measured (and these are usually the ones identified as 'key'), then we:

- Are unlikely to be able to attribute, to the programme, any improvement in an end benefit
- Will not know which parts of the map are working and which are not, and therefore will be unable to remedy any deficiencies
- Will probably have to wait many months, if not years, to know whether or not we have been successful, with no intermediate indication as to whether we are on target – a foolish high-risk approach.

Furthermore, the burden of measurement is rarely as bad as it first appears, because many of the identified measures are often already being tracked or can easily be computed from metrics which are already being captured. Tracking and reporting the new measures may be time-consuming but the extra effort can often be shared among the stakeholders who have a genuine interest in seeing the benefit realized.

Choosing which benefits to measure and examining what constitutes a good measure are explored in more detail, with reference to an illustrative example, in Chapter 13.

5.8 PHASE DOCUMENTS

The documents to be completed in this phase are:

- The stakeholder engagement strategy
- The programme brief.

The issues log and the risk register are ongoing, although extracts from them may appear in the programme brief. In addition, the two documents that should be started during this phase are the blueprint and the benefit realization plan (BRP).

5.8.1 The stakeholder engagement strategy

The stakeholder engagement strategy describes how the programme will engage with stakeholders to motivate them to participate and realize the benefits. It needs to specify:

- Who will lead on particular kinds of engagement
- How stakeholders will be identified, categorized and grouped
- How stakeholders will be engaged – e.g. workshops, focus groups
- How the stakeholder profiles will be populated.

The stakeholder engagement strategy should also include the first attempt at stakeholder identification and grouping (see Figure 5.1).

A fuller treatment of stakeholder engagement is given in MSP.

5.8.2 The programme brief

The programme brief builds on the programme mandate adding further detail, particularly in the following areas:

- **Inclusion of benefit maps**
- **Inclusion of BDMs**
- **Consolidated benefits**

- **Level of stakeholder commitment**
- **Risks and issues**
- Consolidated changes and outline blueprint, validating any solution ideas included in the programme mandate
- High-level analysis of the options available
- Estimated costs and timescales
- Measures for the benefits
- Ideas for programme organization and governance.

The items in bold would probably be mandatory and the remainder, if not available at this stage, would be determined during Phase 3 and presented as part of the business case.

Of these documents, a decision as to whether to proceed to Phase 3 will be based on the programme brief. Any major risks will be included in this document. The stakeholder engagement strategy and the risk register are useful documents to support the management of the programme and, assuming the go-ahead to proceed is given, will be handed over to the programme manager, once appointed.

5.8.3 Blueprint

The blueprint is the document that describes and costs the future business state or target operating model (the 'to be'). This document will often also describe the starting position (the 'as is'). It shows how the new enablers, processes and business changes will integrate together to form the new environment, and should include:

- New enablers, including re-designed processes
- Any required new organizational structures, roles and skills
- Required business changes, including cultural changes.

The document could be structured around objectives and/or functions and may define intermediate states in addition to the start and end states. The set of BDMs describes the future state, structured around objectives, and therefore represents a large part of the blueprint at this interim stage.

A more detailed description of the blueprint, including its design and delivery, is given in Chapter 8 of MSP.

5.8.4 Benefit realization plan

Unlike the benefit management strategy, which may include a plan for the application of BRM, the benefit realization plan (BRP) is the plan for the realization of the set of benefits specific to the particular change initiative. It would normally include:

- The vision
- A strategy map of the objectives, showing the programme boundary
- An alignment check with the organization's mission, direction and any strategic plans for change
- Benefits maps for each of the objectives, selected to bound the programme
- BDMs showing the changes required to realize the benefits
- Consolidation of dependent changes with responsibilities and timescales
- A benefit distribution matrix, showing benefits and disbenefits by stakeholder
- Measures that have been identified for at least the majority of the benefits
- Classification of benefits and/or measures (see section 10.2)
- A set of trajectories for each of the benefit measures

- Responsibilities for benefit delivery (benefit owners) and for tracking (measure monitors)
- A full set of benefit profiles (usually as an appendix).

The BRP is a critical component of the business case at each review point, and the full BRP will become a critical component of the full business case. However, at this stage of the lifecycle, the BRP will be incomplete and therefore just a draft.

5.9 RESOURCE REQUIREMENTS

This phase requires considerably more effort than Phase 1. There may need to be several mapping workshops plus measures workshops and time for further analysis and refinements. With experienced facilitation, a reasonable good quality map can generally be produced in four to five hours by a team of four to six people, with an appropriate mix of representation and skills. If the teams are very familiar with the BRM process one experienced facilitator may be able to facilitate two teams in parallel.

The effort required to undertake this phase is likely to be:

- Eight to 15 days for the benefit facilitator
- One and a half days for each of the stakeholder representatives
- About 15 minutes for the portfolio board.

6 Applying BRM Phase 3: define initiatives

6.1 PHASE CONTENT AND PROCESS

This is a very detailed phase where much of the remainder of the planning and laying of foundations is accomplished. It will continue to require significant stakeholder engagement.

This phase involves:

- A wider and more involved engagement of stakeholders
- Finalizing requirements and completing the blueprint
- Issuing ITTs, if required
- Completing the BRP
- Developing a business case
- Securing approval and funding
- Establishing the programme and project structure
- Organizing resources
- Preparing for benefit tracking and reporting.

The order in which these are performed will depend on the organization, though the above may provide a reasonable chronological order. Where possible, activities may be undertaken in parallel.

6.2 ENGAGING STAKEHOLDERS

As progress continues through the lifecycle, more stakeholders from each of the stakeholder groups are likely to become involved in the process – some through further workshops, others through alternative forms of engagement. It is important to have relevant stakeholder contribution in order to:

- Finalize requirements
- Weight map paths and prioritize solution options
- Develop the blueprint
- Determine measure attributes, including baselines and predicted values
- Take ownership of the benefits
- Commit to measuring and reporting.

So, early in this phase a stakeholder engagement plan should be produced showing when and which stakeholders need to be engaged in each of the above activities.

During this phase, contributions from this programme can be added to the stakeholder profiles, illustrating the relationship between the changes and the stakeholders impacted, including:

- Changes for which they will be responsible
- Changes which they will experience (or which will be imposed upon them).

A stakeholder may be an individual but, more likely, a role or group of roles. The stakeholder profile, which would normally be a single page, contains a consolidation of impacts from the complete portfolio of change initiatives. It would also include the impacts of benefits and disbenefits and any responsibilities for benefit delivery and benefit tracking. The structure of a typical profile is shown in Figure 6.1.

6.3 FINALIZING AND COSTING REQUIREMENTS

By the end of Phase 2, a comprehensive set of requirements – enablers and business changes – should have been identified and consolidated across the set of BDMs.

Stakeholder profile				
Stakeholder role/name				
Benefits to be received				
Ref. no.	Description	Due date		
Disbenefits expected				
Ref. no.	Description	Due date		
Benefits which stakeholder is responsible for achieving				
Ref. no.	Description	Measures	Target	Timescale
Benefits which stakeholder is responsible for tracking and reporting				
Ref. no.	Description	Measures	Target	Timescale
Changes which stakeholder is responsible for delivering				
Ref. no.	Description	Actions	Start date	End date
Changes which stakeholder is likely to experience				
Ref. no.	Description	Actions	Start date	End date

Figure 6.1 Template for a stakeholder profile

Further work on these required changes is now needed in order to:

- Decide which are to be included in the proposed programme
- Specify them in greater detail
- Cost them
- Plan the management of the changes, covering design, build/acquisition and implementation.

This is a very iterative process since cost may be one of the criteria for excluding a requirement. However, it is wasteful to spend time on detailed specifications and costs for those requirements which will clearly be excluded.

6.3.1 Deciding what should be included in the programme

The first step should be to remove:

- Any enablers or business changes that are clearly out of scope
- Any enablers or business changes that are being implemented by another programme or project.

When deciding what should be included and choosing between options, it is worth considering the weighting and scoring process described in section 12.3. At a minimum this will highlight the relative importance of benefits on the left-hand side of the benefits map (see Figure 6.2).

The weightings (percentage contributions on the links) are applied working from the right to the left of the benefits maps. A notional score (e.g. 1,000) is applied to the objective and scores for the benefits are then computed by applying the weightings, again working right to left. This effectively ranks the benefits in terms of their contribution to the bounding objective at the right.

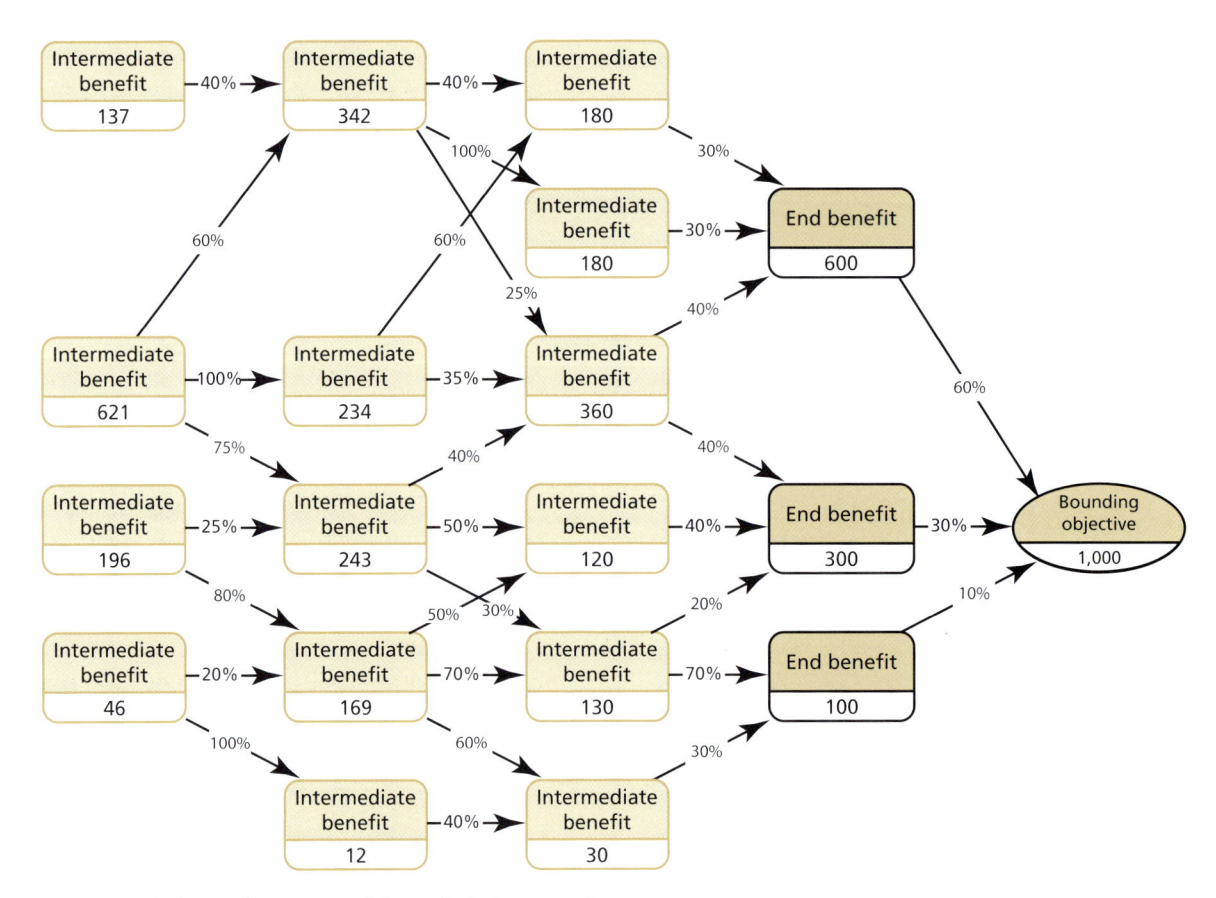

Figure 6.2 Generic benefits map with weightings and scores

This technique can be extremely useful for prioritization and choosing between options but it should always be used alongside other considerations. It does require good quality maps, though, and appropriate stakeholder engagement to determine an agreed set of weightings. Wherever possible the weightings should take account of any relevant hard evidence.

In Figure 6.2, weightings were applied to a benefits map that highlighted which benefits to focus on. However, if the weightings are applied to a BDM instead and continued through to the enablers and changes a more precise analysis of options can be undertaken (as in the next example).

See section 12.3 for more information on weighting.

> A very large public-sector organization embarked on a major transformation programme, beginning with a heavy investment in the application of lean thinking. This resulted in the identification of several hundred improvement opportunities – far more than the organization could resource or fund – and the organization did not know which ones to invest in.
>
> It subsequently applied BRM, with its mapping and weighting techniques, and was able to prioritize and then implement the improvements which would generate the highest value and make the biggest contribution to its strategy.
>
> Further detail on this case is given in section 12.3.

6.3.2 More detailed specification

The whole process of finalizing requirements needs continual stakeholder engagement to guarantee that the results are fit for purpose. To ensure an eventual smooth transition into business as usual, these requirements should be analysed and presented from several different perspectives. The main perspectives and the documents that describe them are:

- Objectives they will deliver and the benefits they will realize – BDMs
- Organizational functions or locations – blueprint
- Specification to supplier – ITT or RFP
- Stakeholders impacted – stakeholder profiles (see section 6.2).

Benefit dependency maps

BDMs have already been described and there is further elaboration in section 12.2. They show how the planned enablers and business changes will deliver the benefits and ultimately the objectives of the programme. By the end of Phase 2 these maps should have been refined with duplicate entities consolidated. Further analysis will determine which parts of the map are out of scope and which changes are being delivered by other initiatives.

The remaining changes should form the basis of the blueprint (a draft version of which would have been produced in Phase 2).

Blueprint

The blueprint is a description of the future business state that the programme needs to deliver in order to fulfil the vision, achieve the objectives and realize the benefits. There may be many different views of this future state, although each should show how the enablers will integrate with the business changes. The future state may be considered:

- By functional unit, describing the before and after states
- By geographic unit, describing the before and after states
- By objective – the BDM.

The outline description, developed in Phase 2, will be completed in this phase as scope is finalized, cross-programme dependencies are identified and options are prioritized and selected. This needs to be complete before issuing ITTs for the delivering of specific enablers.

Invitation to tender or request for proposal

ITTs and RFPs need a precise specification of requirements to enable suppliers to provide good quotations and to facilitate tender analysis. The detail is also likely to become the basis of a legal contract.

When evaluating responses it is important to relate functionality, particularly any that is over and above what was requested, to benefits (see section 7.4).

6.3.3 Costing the changes

The costs of the changes will need to be determined in readiness for the business case. This should include both the costs of the proposed enablers and the required business changes, even if they will be funded differently. Some costs may have to be estimates, until the responses to the ITTs have been received.

It will probably be important not only to determine the total costs but also the cash-flow picture, showing the likely real expenditure by month or quarter.

6.3.4 Planning the management of the changes

Resources need to be organized in the most efficient and effective way in order to deliver the blueprint and, ultimately, the benefits and objectives. Although the delivery structure will depend on the mix of requirements defined, it generally works best when enablers are delivered by projects and the majority of business change is managed and delivered at programme level.

Certainly the division of responsibilities between the component projects and the programme will need to be clearly defined, and this should include how business change is to be coordinated and how any external suppliers are to be managed. This overall structure, including component projects and tranches, should be documented in the programme definition document as part of the recommendations to the end-of-phase review.

6.4 VALIDATING, VALUING AND TRACKING BENEFITS

Validating benefits is more of an implicit (rather than explicit) process. A benefit is valid once:

- A clear description or map path exists showing how the benefit will be realized, including all dependencies – enablers and business changes
- Someone is prepared to own its realization – the benefit owner
- Measures have been determined for the benefit – ideally with baselines, predicted values and improvement timescales.

A benefit profile is a useful document for showing that all of the above exist, and for providing all the information needed by the benefit owner. This profile is a document, ideally a single page, showing all the information relating to a single benefit. A suggested template for the benefit profile is given in Figure 6.3.

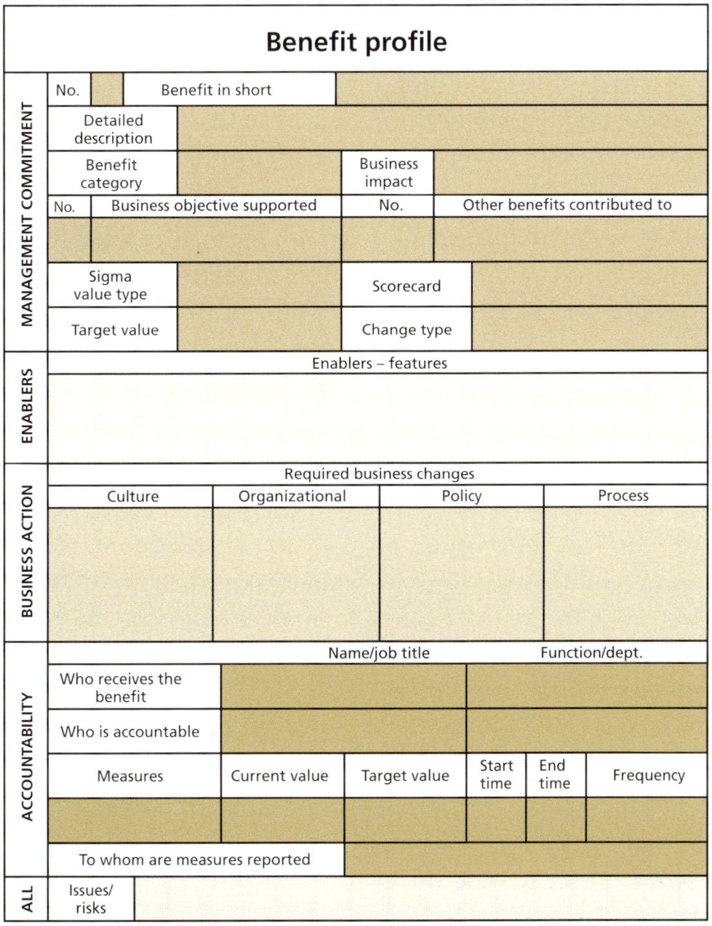

Figure 6.3 Template for a benefit profile

Measures for the consolidated benefits should have been determined in Phase 2. During Phase 3 we must establish a baseline and determine a predicted value (target) for each benefit measure. This will normally be undertaken in measure workshops, working with potential benefit owners and stakeholders who are close to the relevant change activity. Information such as baselines and benchmarks will need to be determined outside the workshop process.

The predicted values will form an important part of the justification or business case and so need to be determined with as much rigour as possible. Each prediction should be the anticipated improvement in the measure, resulting from the programme, and the measure should relate as closely as possible to the wording of the benefit. The majority of predicted values will be expressed in non-financial terms.

Part 2: Applying BRM to programmes and projects

The timing and duration of the improvement will vary from measure to measure and so should, ideally, be expressed as a delivery profile or trajectory. The simplest trajectory will be a straight line running from the baseline to the predicted value over the improvement timescale (see Figure 6.4).

To ensure reasonable rigour, the following points need to be considered when determining predicted values:

- The views of stakeholders close to the action, particularly the potential benefit owners
- The Sigma value type classification of the measures (see section 10.2)
- Any relevant benchmark data
- Current baseline or trend data, if known
- Any known numeric relationships between the benefit in question and its feeder benefits – these can often be determined from existing data within the organization
- The predicted values for the feeder benefits
- The probability of significant influences from outside the programme
- The application of relevant statistical techniques.

Once measures, predicted values and improvement timescales have been agreed, benefit tracking and reporting should commence so that:

- A baseline can be determined if none exists
- Early benefits (quick wins) can be recognized and claimed
- It is more likely to happen – than if we just say we are going to start to measure in six months.

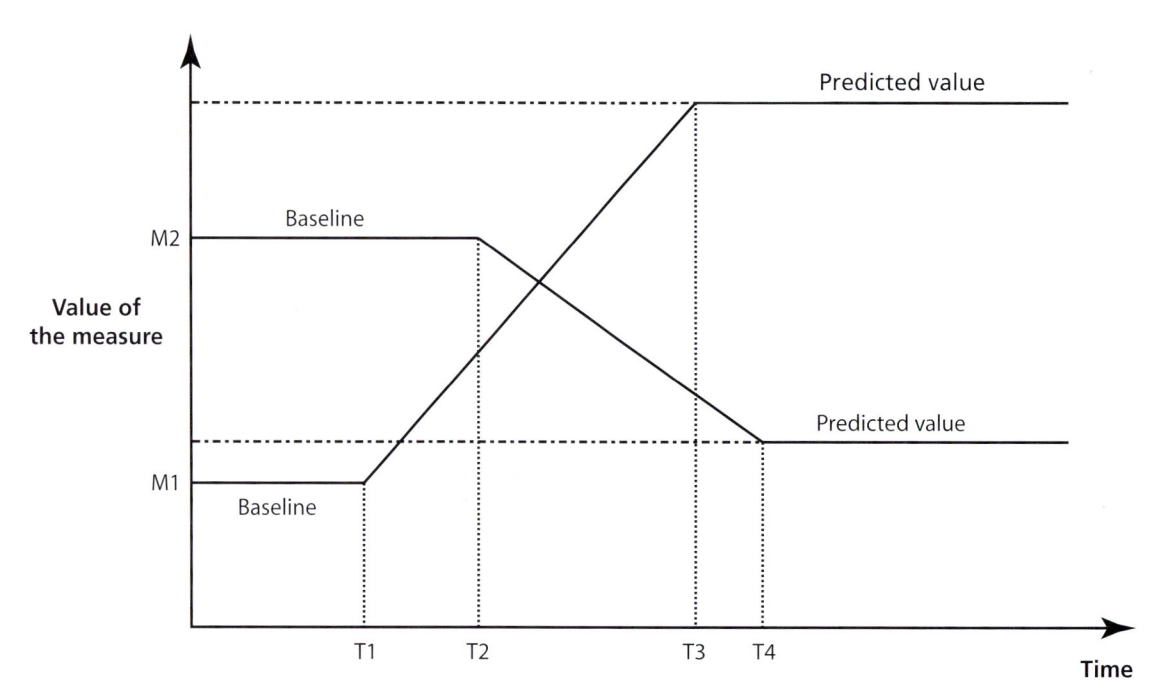

Figure 6.4 Measure baselines and predictions

Even if some of the measures are a bit vague, it is better to start measuring and reporting benefits and to improve the measures later. For reporting with visual impact, apply a colour status (blue, red, amber or green) to each of the benefits on the benefits maps (as described in section 13.7). The degree of tolerance giving rise to amber or red status is a matter for judgement and organizational context.

Reporting will be to both the portfolio and programme boards and to those business stakeholders who have a genuine interest in seeing the benefits realized. An important responsibility of the programme manager is to embed this benefit tracking and reporting regime within the business community, so that when the programme manager moves on benefit tracking and reporting continues. The benefit facilitator can help ensure that this happens.

6.5 DEVELOPING THE BENEFIT REALIZATION PLAN

Because the ultimate purpose of any programme should be the realization of benefits, a key document will be the benefit realization plan (BRP). Its purpose is to:

- Provide the key consolidated information to enable the senior responsible owner (SRO), and the programme manager on behalf of the SRO, to manage the change towards the realization of the benefits
- Inform the business case
- Motivate the stakeholders to embrace the change and take ownership of the tracking and reporting of benefits.

Although this document will have been started in Phase 2 (see section 5.8.4), the programme manager should lead the completion of the BRP, with support from the benefit facilitator and the business change manager, and a significant engagement of stakeholders from the business community.

The structure of the BRP was outlined in section 5.8.4, at the stage when much of the initial information was gathered. Further work on the BRP – filling gaps and elaborating – will be undertaken during this phase.

6.6 DEVELOPING THE PROGRAMME DEFINITION DOCUMENT

The purpose of the programme definition document (PDD) is to provide the consolidated information to enable the programme manager to manage all aspects of the programme and achieve the realization of the benefits. This consolidation needs to summarize rather than duplicate the related documents, such as the blueprint and the BRP.

The programme manager should lead in the creation of the PDD, drawing on the programme brief and risk register and working closely with those engaged in developing the blueprint.

The PDD should include:

- Vision, objectives and a summary of benefits
- Strategy map and possibly a summary BDM (the full set of BDMs will appear in the BRP), highlighting milestones and timescales
- Blueprint summary, including summary of the current state – baselines
- Programme structure, roles and responsibilities
- Resourcing plan
- Programme plan
- Major risks to be managed
- Division of responsibilities between projects and programme

- Stakeholder summary
- Set of benefit profiles (as an appendix).

6.7 DEVELOPING THE BUSINESS CASE

Realizing benefits involves change, and change requires investment, which will need to be justified – this is normally through a business case. The purpose of the business case is to:

- Check that the anticipated return is worth the proposed outlay
- Check that the level of risk is appropriate
- Check the contribution to business strategy
- Check that the proposed investment is worthwhile, relative to other investment options
- Provide the key consolidated information to enable the SRO, and the programme manager on behalf of the SRO, to manage the change towards the realization of the benefits.

The programme manager should lead in the creation of the business case, with support from the benefit facilitator and the business change manager, and significant engagement of stakeholders from the business community.

The business case is a further development of the programme brief (or strategic outline case) but with reasonably firm details, including figures for costs and benefits. It will draw heavily on the content of the BRP and the programme definition document. It is therefore a matter of organizational preference as to whether all three documents are presented to the end-of-phase review board (see section 3.3), thus keeping the business case slim, or cutting and pasting significant parts of the feeder documents into the business case and then only presenting a single document to the review board. See Chapter 14 for further information on documentation.

The suggested minimum content for the business case is:

- A strategy map of objectives, perhaps linked to a vision.
- A matrix showing the programme's expected contribution to the business strategy.
- Expected benefits linked to the necessary transformation and change – through pointers to the maps, which could be included as attachments. This description of how the benefits are to be achieved should be a fundamental part of every business case, although it is often missing.
- The overall risk profile, indicating the major risks to blueprint delivery and benefit realization.
- Estimated costs and timescale.
- The net value of the programme – the difference between the predicted benefit values (financial and non-financial) and the anticipated costs (financial and non-financial), displayed by time period.
- The net present value (NPV) computed from the financial benefit values and costs.
- The NPV computed from the financial and economic benefit values and costs.
- Options that have been considered.
- Portfolio fit, probably using the Cranfield Grid.

6.8 SECURING FUNDING

Mechanisms for securing funding will vary from organization to organization but are usually well established, with specific guidance and clear criteria. However, where a portfolio board exists, it is likely that the business case will be presented to the board, which has the authority to dispense the required funds.

This can be done in two stages – in the first stage the total funds are allocated to the programme and, at the second stage, cases are presented and approved in order to secure the staged release of those funds.

Whatever the approval mechanism, it is vital that sufficient funds are sought covering:

- The anticipated costs of the enablers – generally derived from the responses to the ITTs
- The anticipated costs of the business changes – usually underestimated
- The cost of applying BRM – typically between 4% and 6% of total programme costs.

If only the first of these three is properly funded, then the programme is likely to deliver less than 15% of the potential benefits.

Example

I heard recently of a large public-sector programme where all three costs had been included in the original proposal. But, unfortunately, the approval process lasted over nine months and by the time the approval was given, the cost of the enabler had dramatically increased, leaving nothing for business change or benefit realization. The result is a potentially disastrous situation – for the programme manager, the stakeholders and also the taxpayer.

Worryingly, this is not an isolated incident – similar disasters happen far too often. This publication should help senior managers realize that if business change and benefit realization are not properly funded, benefits are unlikely to be achieved, and so it is irresponsible to throw money away on enablers.

6.9 MOBILIZING RESOURCES

Ideally, Phases 1 and 2 will have been driven and facilitated by the benefit facilitator, with carefully planned involvement of the stakeholders. By Phase 3, the potential programme will have passed two reviews and the likelihood of it becoming formalized as a programme is high. So the time is right to appoint an SRO who then leads in establishing a programme board.

The SRO may be the business manager who has backed the idea through the first two phases and would, ideally, be a senior manager from the stakeholder group which is likely to receive a high proportion of the benefits.

The programme board should comprise senior representatives of the key stakeholders and therefore is likely to include many of the stakeholders who participated in the Phase 1 workshop. The programme board should appoint a programme manager and perhaps a business change manager.

The programme manager should have a good understanding of the business environment and, ideally, come from the business community. It is essential that they have good programme management skills. During this phase, the programme manager will need to work closely with the benefit facilitator.

It is probably best to build up the programme team once the business case has been approved, though the recommended structure, such as the formation of projects within the programme, and roles such as the business change manager, should be proposed in the PDD and probably in the business case too.

For further details about roles, responsibilities and organizational structures, see Chapter 11.

7 Applying BRM Phase 4: optimize initiatives

7.1 PHASE OVERVIEW

During Phase 3:

- The blueprint, necessary to deliver the end goal – objectives and benefits – was defined
- The required changes were costed and the benefits valued
- A business case justifying the investment was prepared and approved
- The programme structure was established
- Many of the resources were recruited.

In summary, a feasible solution has been determined, costed and justified, outline approval has been given, and resources have been secured to deliver this solution.

Without fundamentally changing what has been approved, Phase 4 seeks to leverage more benefits by applying benefit-led decision making in several areas:

- Through continuing stakeholder engagement
- By checking focus and alignment
- By optimizing the solution
- By optimizing the implementation.

Once this has been done, this phase focuses on:

- Selling the changes and promoting the BRP
- Establishing a benefit tracking and reporting regime within the business.

7.2 STAKEHOLDER ENGAGEMENT

Stakeholder engagement continues throughout the phase, in accordance with the stakeholder engagement plan. A core group of knowledgeable and influential stakeholders will help with:

- Checking focus and alignment
- Optimizing the solution and its implementation
- Developing and owning the benefit tracking and reporting process.

The BRP should be promoted among a much wider group of stakeholders to spread understanding and to motivate stakeholders to participate positively in the change process.

7.3 CHECKING ALIGNMENT, INTERNAL CONSISTENCY AND BALANCE

It is well worth checking to see if the Cranfield Grid classification of the programme, as used to check portfolio balance in Phase 1 (Figure 4.5), is consistent with the distribution of benefits using a similar framework. Figure 7.1 highlights a possible, but not uncommon, inconsistency between the application of the two classifications.

If the investment classification in Figure 7.1 is correct then the big prize should be a set of strategic benefits – which have not been identified and so are very unlikely to be realized. This highlights an enormous missed opportunity and a largely wasted investment – an all too common situation. This unfortunate situation is generally a result of:

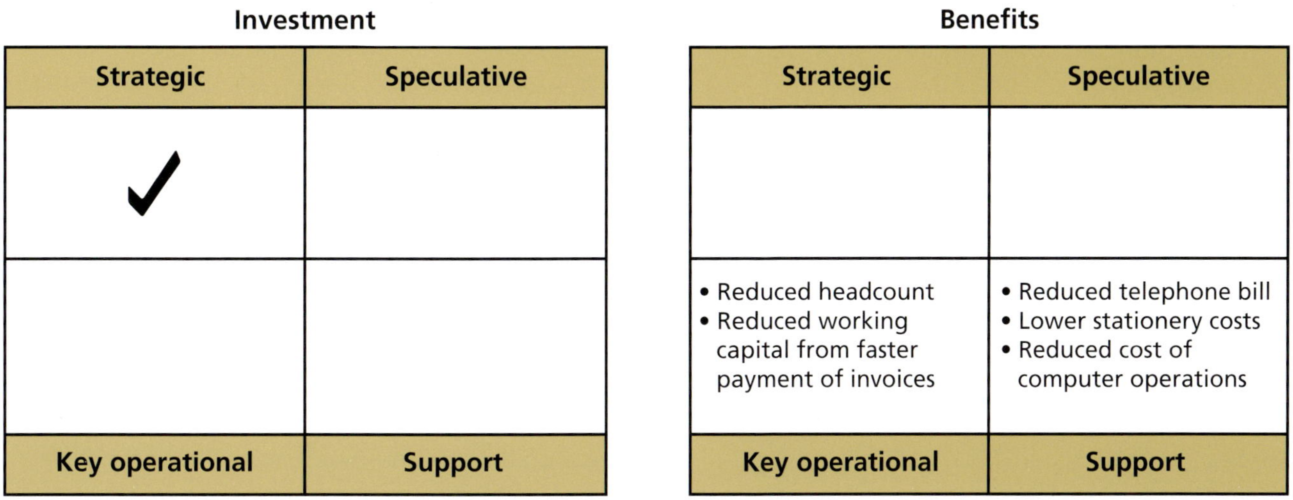

Applying BRM Phase 4: optimize initiatives | 51

Investment	
Strategic	**Speculative**
✓	
Key operational	**Support**

Benefits	
Strategic	**Speculative**
• Reduced headcount • Reduced working capital from faster payment of invoices	• Reduced telephone bill • Lower stationery costs • Reduced cost of computer operations
Key operational	**Support**

Figure 7.1 Misalignment of investment and benefit classifications

Table 7.1 IAM showing benefits by value type and business impact

Sigma value type		Business impact			
		Speculative	Strategic	Key operational	Support
Definite	Financial			Reduced salary costs	Reduced telephone bill
	Non-financial			Greater administrative productivity	
Expected	Financial		Increased sales revenue from other products		
	Non-financial		Improved responsiveness to clients		
Logical	Financial		Improved management of risk		
	Non-financial		Greater customer satisfaction		
Intangible		Improved image Increased client confidence			

- A lack of engagement of the most appropriate stakeholders – those who think creatively and strategically
- Stakeholders consciously or sub-consciously filtering out the benefits which do not have obvious hard financial values – and many of the strategic benefits cannot meaningfully be given hard financial values.

The alternative interpretation of this misalignment is where the programme is actually a support programme but has been misclassified as strategic. This means that:

- The portfolio balance becomes distorted
- Expectations are mismanaged
- The scarce resource of a programme manager capable of managing a strategic programme is wasted.

Using these two applications of the Cranfield Grid to check for consistency will quickly highlight any of the above problem situations and enable remedial action to be taken.

There are many other checks that can easily be undertaken using an investment assessment matrix (IAM). An IAM is a matrix where the horizontal and vertical axes are two different attributes taken from the benefit profile, and the body of the matrix is populated with programme benefits. These visuals can be used to:

Table 7.2 IAM showing benefits by beneficiary and by business impact

	Public	Magistrates court	DVLA	Police	Government
Speculative	Improved public perception				Less call on legal aid
Strategic	Fewer dangerous drivers on the road Improved sentencing	Fewer adjournments More up-to-date information		More remands Improved sentencing	
Key operational		Reduced duplication Fewer interruptions for staff Improved staff productivity Lower court costs	Quicker turnaround Reduced duplication	Faster access to DVLA information Reduced duplication	
Support		Less document handling Reduced postage/fax costs	Less document handling		

- Check for consistency
- Check for balance
- Communicate expectations.

Tables 7.1, 7.2 and 7.3 illustrate how an IAM can be used.

The matrix in Table 7.1, which shows the distribution of benefits for an insurance company programme that was moving it towards a call-centre approach, provides a consistency check because benefits would not be expected to lie outside the shaded area. The horizontal axis represents the Cranfield Grid classification, and the vertical axis the Sigma value classification; both are attributes of the benefit as shown in the benefit profile.

Table 7.2 shows the distribution of benefits for a highways project, looking at beneficiary and business impact using the Cranfield Grid classifications. This business impact classification is very useful when considering the relative significance of benefits –

Table 7.3 IAM showing benefits by change type and value type

Sigma value type	Change type			
		Doing new things	Doing things better	Stop doing things
Definite	Financial			Reduced telephone bill
				Reduced salary costs
	Non-financial		Greater administrative productivity (e.g. fewer errors)	
Expected	Financial		Increased sales of other products	
	Non-financial		Improved responsiveness to clients	
Logical	Financial	Improved management of risk		
	Non-financial	Increased client confidence		
Intangible			Improved image	

for example, when comparing the strategic benefit of 'fewer dangerous drivers on the road' with the support benefit of 'reduced postage/fax costs'.

Table 7.3 is useful for checking whether there is an appropriate balance between the three columns, prompting the question: 'Are we transforming enough, or are we just automating the status quo?'

Tables 7.1, 7.2 and 7.3 are also useful for communicating expectations and can be generated directly from the set of benefit profiles without additional information gathering. So, with appropriate software, they can all be generated automatically.

7.4 OPTIMIZING THE SOLUTION

By the end of Phase 3 we should have established that, in some cases, a feasible technical solution exists whose cost is such that a business case was made and approved. Sometimes, there might be more than one solution; sometimes there might be none.

Within this phase we can explore variations or alternative solutions which may yield better returns. This consideration will begin when the responses to the ITTs are received. In particular we will need to consider what additional benefits might be enabled from any functionality, offered by those tendering, which is over and above that which was specified in the ITT.

In this kind of exploration it may be useful to produce a matrix relating enabler features to benefits, as shown in Table 7.4.

The matrix in Table 7.4 should prompt questions like: 'Do we need to purchase Feature F3?' Even when the response is that F3 comes as part of a total package, it is important to ensure that resource is not wasted in:

- Setting up the feature and getting it to work, or
- Training people how to use the feature.

Table 7.4 Relationship between enabler features and benefits

System features	Benefits					
	B1	B2	B3	B4	B5	B6
Planned						
F1	✔					
F2		✔	✔			✔
F3						
F4		✔			✔	
F5	✔				✔	✔
Potential						
PF1		✔	✔			
PF2						
PF3	✔					✔

Benefits should be used to:

- Optimize the required functionality (e.g. in comparing bids)
- Set up technology
- Focus training
- Sequence data load
- Sequence roll-out.

If a package of change is being rolled out over a number of sites it will probably need to be sequenced for practical reasons and therefore spread over a longish time period. Where several hundred sites are involved, roll-out may take between 18 months and 2 years. In these situations it is important to use benefit considerations to determine, or at least influence, the roll-out sequence.

> **Example**
>
> One organization had implemented a new procurement system and needed to backload a lot of existing data, such as supplier details. This data was of variable quality and needed cleaning before loading to the new system. Therefore, data migration was managed as a phased process. The project team chose to start with those suppliers who provided occasional high-value products. They were then able to demonstrate to the sponsor rapid progress when they reported progress by purchase value. This was not a benefit-driven strategy since the big benefits came from the high-volume, low-value purchases.

7.5 PROMOTING THE BRP

Once the optimizations (see section 7.4) are complete and plans are finalized, they need to be communicated and stakeholders motivated to participate positively in the change process. A powerful vehicle for securing this buy-in should be the BRP, refined and updated to reflect any of the optimizations agreed during the earlier part of this phase.

The BRP may need to be packaged in bite-sized bits to communicate appropriately to different stakeholders.

7.6 ESTABLISHING BENEFIT TRACKING AND REPORTING

An important part of this phase is establishing comprehensive benefit tracking and reporting.

Benefits and their measures were identified in Phase 2. Baselines, predicted values and benefit owners were determined in Phase 3 and the tracking of some benefits should also have started in Phase 3, since it is generally recommended that the tracking and reporting of benefits should commence as soon as the measures have been determined, as this:

- Increases the probability of it happening
- Provides baseline information if none exists
- Detects early benefits or quick wins.

Early benefits often arise as stakeholders, engaged through a workshop process, start to work and behave differently. By detecting these quick wins through early benefit tracking they can often be claimed and put to the credit of the programme.

With the major changes about to commence, this phase should create a comprehensive benefit tracking process, incorporating any monitoring which has already begun. For reasons outlined in section 13.5, it needs to cover the majority of benefits identified in the set of BDMs.

Overall the tracking mechanism should:

- Monitor progress through the whole change lifecycle to the eventual realization of the end benefits and the achievement of the objectives
- Give an early indication of any part of the map that is not working as intended, so that remedial action might be taken
- Meet the needs of the different stakeholders involved
- Spread the measurement load between interested stakeholders
- Utilize visual communication such as dashboards and maps – the latter with BRAG status applied (see section 13.7)
- Enable reporting to the portfolio board, using a consistent format, as agreed for the organization
- Be suitable for transferring, to the business community, responsibility for benefit tracking.

7.7 RESOURCE REQUIREMENTS

This phase will be led by the programme manager, with some support from the benefit facilitator, and will continue to involve stakeholders, as indicated in section 7.2.

Overall, the BRM activities are not very labour intensive though the elapsed time may be significant since this is the phase when the enablers are developed and built. Whether these are built internally or by an external supplier their development needs to be properly managed from within the programme and they are generally best set up as projects within the programme.

8 Applying BRM Phase 5: manage initiatives

8.1 FOUNDATIONS FOR CHANGE

Phase 5 is where the main changes will occur – enablers will be delivered and business changes implemented to deliver the new business state based on the blueprint. This phase may require a significant proportion of the total programme budget and will require strong leadership and careful management to minimize resistance to change and achieve a smooth transition into business as usual.

This phase is easier when the original idea for the change comes from the business community and where the importance of the business change is recognized as a critical success factor for the realization of benefits.

The success of this phase will largely depend on how well foundations have been laid during earlier phases, including:

- Initial commitment by senior stakeholders
- Maintaining effective stakeholder engagement throughout the lifecycle
- Early identification of disbenefits
- Recognizing and appropriately filling key business change roles
- Fully budgeting for the business change within the business case
- Ensuring that the funding for the business change is not diverted to fund deficits in other areas – e.g. if the cost of the enabler overruns.

8.2 ROLES AND RESPONSIBILITIES

There are several roles that contribute to the success of this phase, including:

- The SRO and the programme board
- The programme manager
- The business change manager
- Change champions
- Benefit owners
- The benefit facilitator.

Achieving the new business state, as per the blueprint, is likely to require change in many parts of the organization and often in functions outside of the organization. So, as senior managers within the various stakeholder groups, the members of the programme board have a key responsibility – encouraging and supporting the required changes within the functions for which they are responsible. The SRO, as chair and probably the most senior member of the programme board, may also need to influence the stakeholder groups outside the organization.

The programme manager must continue to ensure cohesion between those delivering and implementing the enablers (the enabler project managers) and the person overseeing the business change (the business change manager). This responsibility will cover:

- Minimizing the impact of disbenefits
- Acceptance testing of the enablers
- Piloting implementation
- Acceptance testing of the piloted new business state

- Sequencing the full roll-out, taking account of the need to optimize benefit realization without overwhelming any stakeholder group
- The handover of responsibilities to the business community.

The role of business change manager is critical. It requires good leadership and motivational skills and, ideally, a good track record for managing change. For a project or small programme this role may be absorbed by the programme manager, provided they have the necessary skills; for a significant programme, however, this is likely to be a full-time role distinct from the programme manager.

As early as possible the business change manager needs to co-opt local support in each of the business units where significant change will be required. These individuals are the change champions and their role (which is likely to be in addition to their day jobs) will be more like that of an ambassador or evangelist.

Benefit owners, who are responsible for the realization of specific benefits, have a particular interest in seeing the changes introduced smoothly and on time. They will need to encourage and support the change champions, and may often be a change champion themselves.

The benefit facilitator is unlikely to be heavily involved during this phase but should maintain a watching brief, not least to validate the accuracy of the BDMs whose construction they facilitated.

8.3 OVERCOMING RESISTANCE TO CHANGE

With good stakeholder engagement through the earlier phases, resistance should be reduced, though it will depend on the significance of the disbenefits. Sometimes the general resistance to change may intensify, especially when a particular stakeholder sees only disbenefits. This situation calls for focused attention and creative responses. A structured and focused response is illustrated in the next example, in which a computer company is experiencing a downturn in profits.

Example

A computer company had grown rapidly to become a significant international player but, having recently fallen out of favour, it was quickly losing market share, and consequently profits were falling. Its growth had been achieved largely by setting tough targets linked to attractive bonuses, and then making these targets tougher year on year. The sales people were committed to achieving their bonuses – it was not uncommon for expensive family holidays to be planned in anticipation of the additional remuneration. The bonus targets were related to the orders received – in itself a bad choice of target (see section 13.4). As the targets grew tougher, corners were cut and customers were often sold equipment which poorly matched their needs – sometimes the initial installation did not even work without replacing solution components.

Naturally, management was concerned and the IT director proposed a project which involved building a knowledge-based system to help the sales force model client requirements, using checklists to ensure the workability of any proposed solution. As part of the project, the sales force would be provided with laptops and trained in the new system, and in the new ways of working. The sales force could see only difficulties and resisted the change. They recognized they would have to take training time out from selling, change their whole approach, and would be constrained in the range of options offered. Consequently, they did not believe they could achieve their targets. Figure 8.1 helped to assess the situation, focus effort and determine some actions.

Considering the benefits expected from the project by the primary stakeholders, it is easy to see that the sales force, with their short-term focus, saw no benefits. This did not go unnoticed by the senior managers, who then recognized the need to change the reward structure for the sales people, rewarding sales only when they led to error-free system configurations.

This process may appear rather bureaucratic, so it is worth noting that the generation of the content of at least the first three columns of Figure 8.1 required little effort, since this information should already exist in the benefit profiles, or in the BRM database if software is used. The anticipated resistance is easily deduced and recognizes the fact that, although senior managers saw the need for a new incentive model, some felt the proposal was complicated and uncertain, whereas the existing system was tried and tested.

The programme manager, realizing that only two of the five stakeholders were showing resistance, could focus on these two stakeholders, making best use of limited resources. The programme manager examined the current and required levels of commitment from these stakeholders and determined actions to motivate the change.

Stakeholder group	Perceived benefits	Changes needed	Anticipated resistance	Level of commitment (C=Current, R=Required)				
				Anti	None	Let it happen	Help it happen	Make it happen
Customers	More customer needs met	None	None					
Senior business management	Improved company reputation for quality products	Provide incentives to sales for error-free system configuration	Reluctance to change reward structures		C	Actions? →		R
Sales reps.	None	Use new system when quoting	Extra time and effort when quoting		C	Actions? →	R	
Technical support	Less and easier configuration checking	None	None					
IT developers	More interesting development work	Develop and implement new system	None					

Figure 8.1 *Overcoming stakeholder resistance*

8.4 TRANSITION INTO BUSINESS AS USUAL

This transition is often badly managed, with the programme team dispersing or moving on before the transition to business as usual is fully complete. MSP recognizes the challenge of this transition and to increase focus on this activity has defined three stages:

- Pre-transition
- Transition
- Post-transition.

These three stages are described in detail in MSP, along with suggested responsibilities for each stage.

As with the handover of a baton in a relay race, if the handover to business as usual is not fully accomplished in a smooth and timely manner success will not be within the team's grasp. For the transition to work well, the programme team should engage with the business from an early stage and throughout the lifecycle, carefully planning the transition during Phase 4 and implementing it in Phase 5.

9 Applying BRM Phase 6: manage performance

9.1 BENEFIT TRACKING

The process of benefit tracking should be well established by this stage and is likely to have already reported the full realization of some of the early intermediate benefits.

The challenge in this phase is to ensure total ownership, by the business, of the reporting mechanism, so that when the programme formally closes, an appropriate level of benefit tracking and reporting will continue. This will need to continue at least until the programme's ultimate goals (vision, objectives and benefits) have been achieved.

During this period the values of benefit measures should be reported to:

- Benefit owners, who may be tracking the benefits themselves
- Other relevant stakeholders within the business
- The portfolio board
- The programme board, until it is formally closed.

9.2 ACTING ON MISSED TARGETS

At any stage in the lifecycle, if the achievement of a predicted value is missed by a significant margin (perhaps more than 20%), then the shortfall should be investigated in order to:

- Determine and instigate any simple remedial actions
- Learn lessons, particularly if it is now felt that the predicted value was over ambitious
- Identify and propose a new change initiative to deliver the shortfall.

During this phase, responsibility for the above actions must gradually pass, in a managed fashion, from the programme manager to the business.

9.3 CAPTURING LESSONS LEARNED

It is important to capture any lessons from the programme experience, particularly those that have an impact on benefit realization, but it is equally important to ensure that these lessons are shared so that others may learn from them. In this context, the benefit facilitator has an important role. Lessons learned may arise from:

- Failure to achieve the predicted values for the benefit measures within the expected timeframe
- A formal post-programme review
- The experiences of the programme manager, the business change manager or other members of the programme team.

9.4 CLOSING THE PROGRAMME

It is important that there is a formal closure for the programme, although this should not be scheduled too early. The closure should take place after the new business state, described in the blueprint, has been fully achieved and after many of the intermediate benefits have been realized.

Example

My work for one organization required the frequent use of meeting rooms of varying sizes. As the organization had recently completed a programme to create a modern, cohesive and efficient working environment for staff, in a new purpose-built building, this should not have been a problem. The building included a large complex of meeting rooms of varying sizes, and dates for my meetings were known six weeks in advance. However, no rooms were available for most of these meetings and, as a result, rooms were frequently hired elsewhere, and some two-day events had to be split between different buildings.

Had the programme underestimated the demand and the new offices been built with insufficient meeting facilities? Not at all. Investigation revealed that the majority of meeting rooms were empty on most days, including on those days when external facilities were hired. Staff were block-booking rooms well into the future, in case they were required, but were either not using them or were using large rooms for small meetings.

The programme had failed to provide policies and guidance on the use of rooms, and to put in place necessary procedures and systems. Addressing the problem at such a late stage of the programme lifecycle required the initiation of a new small project, incorporating enablers such as policies, systems and business change to embed them in the working practices of the organization.

Once all the staff were in the new building the SRO declared the programme closed and shortly afterwards benefit reporting ceased. At that stage, not only were the new facilities not being used appropriately, but vacated old buildings had not been sold or re-let. I wondered whether the SRO understood about their accountability for benefits.

This perhaps illustrates one of the differences between a project and programme – where a project usually finishes when its products have been delivered (the new building in this case example) but a programme persists until the changes are embedded and the benefits realized.

Part 3
Elaboration of key techniques and responsibilities

10 Definition, classification and validation of benefits

10.1 DEFINITIONS – BENEFITS AND RELATED ENTITIES

A critical success factor for effective realization of benefits is quality communication. This begins with a clear definition of terms and a precise use of language, and can be enhanced with appropriate use of the visual – diagrams, tables, maps and consistent use of colour.

In relation to change, a benefit is **an outcome of change perceived as positive by a stakeholder**. It is not the change itself that is the activity which requires resource, is scheduled into projects and programmes and has a cost. It is the outcome of this change – provided the outcome is seen as positive by relevant stakeholders. This definition has been found to be very effective in recognizing the full range of benefits and in facilitating their achievement. Many outcomes will be seen as negative and these are referred to as disbenefits.

Since a benefit is an outcome of change, implying a before and after state, a benefit description should start with an adjective indicating the direction of improvement, such as *increased*, *reduced*, *fewer*, *greater*, *less*, *improved*. The discipline of using this form of wording helps to eliminate vague thinking and is a good first step towards measure identification.

A disbenefit is **an outcome of change perceived as negative by a stakeholder**. Therefore, it is not a current problem that the proposed project or programme is trying to fix but rather a new negative situation potentially arising from the proposed programme. It often has an emotional dimension and is based on the perception of the relevant stakeholder. Although this perception is normally founded in reality, the view can often be distorted or exaggerated. As a result, disbenefits can often be reduced by healthy and understanding dialogue.

Some organizations would include 'increased running costs' as a disbenefit. However, it is preferable to see these included in the financial justification for the programme and not treated as disbenefits – although for stakeholders outside the organization making the investment, treating any increased running cost as a disbenefit may be the best solution.

An objective is closely related to a benefit but there is an important difference:

- An objective is **an answer to the important 'why' question and defines purpose, aim, and direction**. A recommended wording discipline is to write all objectives starting with the word 'to'.
- A benefit defines the prize at the end of the journey.

An objective might be 'to increase sales' and the journey (change activity) could be expected to last three years, with the end prize being 'increased sales'. Based on the recommended word structures, 'increase sales' is neither an objective nor a benefit; it is written like an activity or an action but it is so broad that it is unclear what the specific action is.

If an objective is 'to eliminate duplication' the related benefit is best described as 'less duplication' with a target of zero duplication. Like most benefits this is likely to change gradually, steadily reducing duplication, and even if the target is not achieved there could be a significant reduction in duplication, which would be a valuable benefit in itself.

Since a benefit is an outcome of change it is dependent on the effective implementation of the appropriate change. Change is an activity, within and sometimes outside of the organization, which creates new ways of functioning – in particular, new ways of working, new ways of communicating and new ways of making decisions. It normally comprises a combination of two elements, generally referred to as enablers and business changes, where:

- An enabler is **something that can be developed/built/acquired from outside the organization in which it will be embedded and where the benefits will be realized**
- A business change is **a change which occurs within the business/operational environment, such as a new way of working, often embedding an enabler within the organization and culture**.

Another term which is quite often used is 'capability'. This can refer to an enabler or to the integration of enablers and business changes (a sub-state of the blueprint) – for example, new staff (enablers) are trained and developed (business change) to become a skilled team (capability).

In the context of benefit realization a practical definition of a measure is **the entity whose value is reported regularly to demonstrate the realization of the benefit**. It is normally computed from a combination of metrics (the raw data) often collected automatically by the organization – for example, a call centre may automatically capture the start and end time of each call, the number of rings before the call is answered and the time before a caller speaks to a call handler. From these metrics, many measures may be computed, including:

- The average response time (time to speak to a person) per month
- The longest response time each month
- The median response time
- The average response time for each hour of the week.

If other metrics were recorded by the call handler (e.g. whether the caller's query had been resolved by the end of the call), further measures may be computed, such as the average time to query-resolution.

In a business context we consider mainly benefits which are of value to the organization and which are measurable. In relation to a measure, we can regard a benefit as **the improvement in a measure arising from a specific project or programme**.

The term 'goal' is often used in the context of change and therefore needs to be defined. However, with 'vision', 'objectives' and 'benefits' there are already sufficient words to describe the purpose of a change initiative, so instead of trying to identify a distinctly different characteristic for the target, it is better to use 'goal' as a generic term for any of the above. A goal is **a general term for the purpose of change which may be any combination of vision, objectives and benefits**.

10.2 BENEFIT CLASSIFICATION

This section summarizes a range of frequently used benefit classifications, some of which have already been introduced in Part 2.

There are several reasons why it is useful to classify benefits, including:

- Communicating and managing expectations
- Analysing the impact of a programme or project
- Simplifying the identification of duplicate benefits
- Checking for balance and alignment
- Assessing the degree of transformation
- Facilitating portfolio management.

Five commonly used classifications are:

- By beneficiary
- By business impact
- By Sigma value type
- By category (family grouping)
- By change type.

10.2.1 By beneficiary

A useful output from early workshops is a benefit distribution matrix showing benefits and disbenefits by stakeholder impacted. An example was given in Figure 5.6.

Figure 5.6 is useful for understanding the distribution of benefits and disbenefits by stakeholder and highlights potential problem areas – where stakeholders may not be sufficiently motivated to engage in the process and manage the business change which falls in their area. Once highlighted, it will be important to spend time with these stakeholders to explore their perception of the disbenefits they feel they will experience.

While most disbenefits are based on reality, the perception of this reality may be exaggerated or distorted – for example, in Figure 5.6 business users feel negative about the extra effort they are now being asked to invest in benefit workshops. While it is true that they are being asked to give up time to focus on benefits, which is something they didn't do in the past, it is likely to save them a lot of time later in the lifecycle, so there may be no overall increase in effort. In addition it would deliver them a much better result.

10.2.2 By business impact

There are many ways to assess business impact but the two assessments which are most frequently applied use three and four categorizations of benefits respectively.

The first categorizes benefits according to their contribution to:

- Internal improvement – for example, efficiency benefits
- The organization's growth
- Risk reduction for the organization.

The second is based on the Cranfield Grid and categorizes benefits based on the definition in four quadrants (see Figure 4.5).

As well as using the template in Figure 4.5 to classify and check alignment and balance, it can also be used to aid benefit identification. In MSP there is an example of this grid being used for higher-level analysis.

10.2.3 By Sigma value type

Benefits are often referred to as tangible or intangible, hard or soft, quantifiable or qualitative – yet there seems no uniform understanding of what these words actually mean. Furthermore, the language implies in each instance that there are only two states. In fact, there is a spectrum of benefit value types and using just two words ignores useful distinguishing information.

Sigma value type		Definition	Example	
			Financial/cashable	Non-financial/non-cashable
Tangible	Definite	Value may be predicted with confidence or certainty – not affected by external factors	Reduced costs	Fewer steps in a process
	Expected	Value may be predicted on the basis of someone else's experience or based on historic trends	Increased sales	Quicker performance of tasks
	Logical	Logically, a benefit may be anticipated whose value may be measured but not predicted	Improved management of insurance risk	Greater customer satisfaction
Intangible		May be anticipated but difficult to substantiate	Improved image	

Figure 10.1 Sigma value types

With just two types, if organizations give little or no attention to the second type of benefit and they use a narrow definition for the first type, a large number of valuable benefits are likely to be ignored, which is a serious yet common problem.

One effective way to address these issues is to adopt the Sigma value type classification illustrated in Figure 10.1. The seven states in this framework overcome the ambiguity and bluntness of the two-state options, clarify the distinction between tangible and intangible, and separate it from the distinction between financial and non-financial.

For a benefit to be financial it must describe either an increase of money flowing in through the door or a decrease in money flowing out through the door. Other distinctions distort the truth and carry significant risk, often resulting in confusion and wasted investment.

This framework can be applied to both benefits and measures. It has been used effectively, often within the context of a business case, by many organizations over the past 20 years and was included in the 2007 edition of MSP (Table 7.2).

There is a frequent drive, in both public and private sectors, to try to put a financial value on most, if not all, benefits, but this can be extremely dangerous. To understand why this could be dangerous let us consider the benefit 'fewer steps in a process'. This is a non-financial benefit which would be measured by the number of steps in the

Definition, classification and validation of benefits | 69

process. This measure can have a baseline (say 50 steps), a target or predicted value (say 35 steps), and an improvement timescale (say 18 months). The value of the benefit is therefore 15 fewer steps.

Frequently, people will say that it is possible to put a financial value on this benefit. The partial benefits map (see Figure 10.2) helps us to explore the thinking behind this assertion. In this map, based on the earlier definition, the only two financial benefits are highlighted in darker shading.

When people assert that Benefit 1 can be given a financial value, they are usually thinking about the path from Benefit 1 through Benefits 3 and 7 to Benefit 11. There are four important reasons why Benefit 1 should not be given a financial value:

- The intended path (from Benefit 1 through Benefits 3 and 7 to Benefit 11) should not be assumed within a benefit value calculation but be made explicit and documented so that later there is no misunderstanding about the intention.
- The day the target for 'fewer steps' is reached will not be the same day that 'reduced salary costs' is achieved – these times could be at least six months apart. Each benefit should have its own target and timescale and be independently monitored to see that it is achieved.
- Even if the separate targets and timescales are recognized, it may not necessarily be a question of just waiting six months to realize the financial benefit, there may be activity, such as

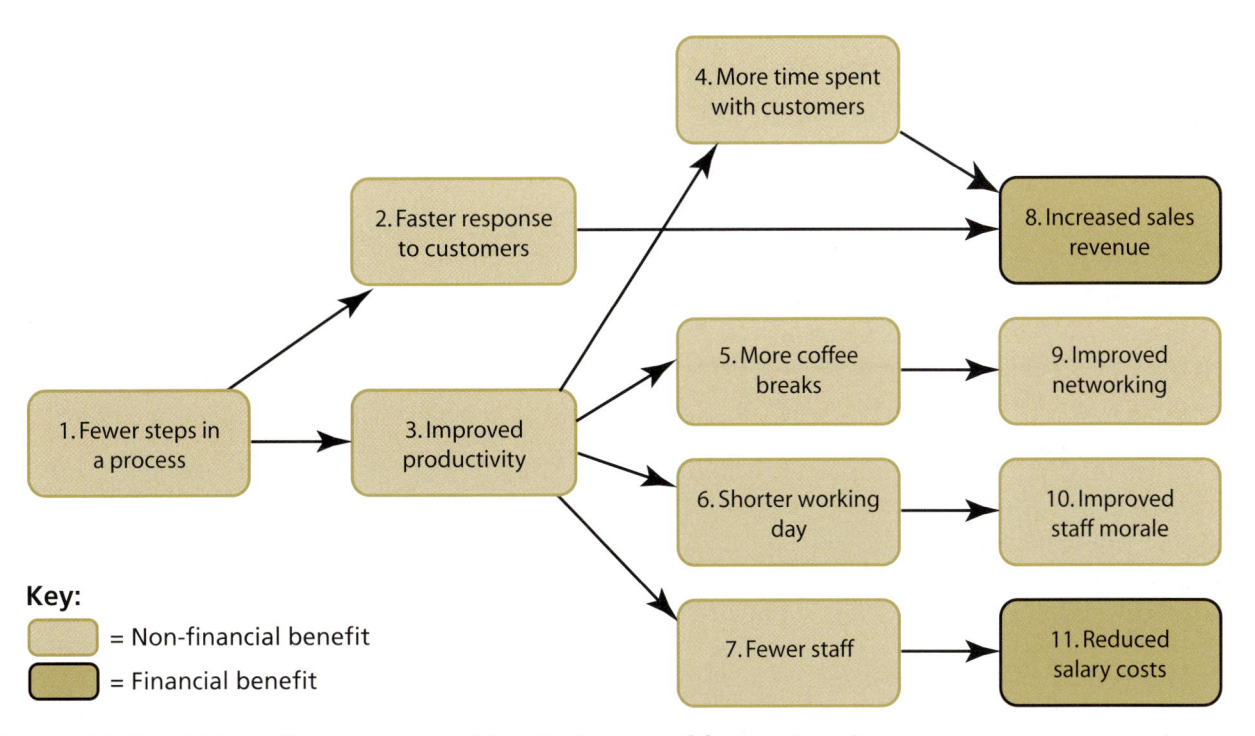

Figure 10.2 Partial benefits map to consider the impact of fewer steps in a process

business change, which is necessary to move from one to the other.

- If 'fewer steps' is given a financial value there is a risk that 'reduced salary costs' is also given a financial value and that they get added together – leading to double counting.

Figure 10.2 illustrates a very real and frequently occurring problem, where the outcome from a project team activity is inappropriately given a financial value. The project team does a good job and delivers the 'fewer steps'; the box is ticked and, after the celebrations, the project team moves on to their next job. In most cases no financial benefits will actually be realized, because:

- The necessary path had not been visibly mapped out and documented.
- The financial value was put in the wrong place.
- No one was given responsibility for following the path through after the project team had delivered their bit. This further activity could be managed within a programme which includes the said project, or within business as usual.

Maps, such as the one in Figure 5.6, are extremely useful for considering options and then communicating expectations. A participant in one of the groups with whom this map was shared, said that it closely resembled a recent project, which didn't have such a map. In this project there was a major clash between the sales director and the finance director. The sales director was expecting all of the benefits in increased sales and the finance director all of the benefits in reduced salary costs. Clearly they couldn't both have the whole of the cake, but they could share it. In order to share the benefits, it is best to discuss the basis for this at the outset and then communicate and manage accordingly.

In the example illustrated in Figure 10.2, management must agree and communicate their intentions regarding 'improved productivity'. The logic of the map shows that there are four feasible options, but management might choose to reject the option for more coffee breaks and distribute the time saved between the other three, for example:

- More time with customers (30%)
- Shorter working day (20%)
- Fewer staff (50%).

The map can then be used to communicate these intentions.

10.2.4 By category

Categorizations based on the characteristics of the benefit can also be useful, such as:

- Reduced costs
- Increased revenue
- Reduced risk
- Improved productivity
- Better equipped workforce
- Increased staff motivation
- Better customer service
- Improved image
- Strategic positioning.

A similar kind of categorization is suggested in Table 7.3 of the MSP guidance and listed here:

- Policy or legal requirement (mandatory)
- Quality of service
- Internal improvement
- Process improvement (productivity or efficiency)
- Personnel or HR management
- Risk reduction
- Flexibility
- Economy

- Revenue enhancement or acceleration
- Strategic fit.

Many organizations have their own defined categories, which all projects and programmes have to use.

This kind of categorization is useful for comparing programmes and projects across the portfolio. It can also be useful for putting a large number of benefits into groups prior to the identification of duplicates.

10.2.5 By change type

A further classification, which is used to assess whether the programme or project is likely to deliver the required degree of transformation, considers whether the benefits arise from:

- Doing current activities a little bit better
- Undertaking new activities
- Stopping activities.

10.3 BENEFIT VALIDATION

Benefits often appear in programme and project documents which are not necessarily valid. They may represent good ideas and relevant wishes but more is needed for them to be valid. For a benefit to be valid:

- There must be a clear description or map showing the logic of how the benefit will be achieved
- The required changes must have been scheduled within the project/programme structure
- There must be someone who is prepared to own it and take responsibility for its realization
- Measures must be determined for it, ideally with baselines, predicted values, and improvement timescales.

10.4 BENEFIT VALUATION

All benefits should be valued in terms which are as close as possible to the way the benefit or its measure is described – for example, in section 10.2.3 the benefit 'fewer steps in a process' was valued as '15 fewer steps' which was the expected improvement in the measure.

There is a strong tendency to try to value all benefits in financial terms. As mentioned above, this carries many risks including:

- It is often artificial
- It can be very misleading
- It frequently leads to double counting
- It distorts the truth.

So why is there such pressure to undertake this, often artificial, conversion? It occurs for two main reasons:

- To justify some proposed expenditure
- To compare and choose between options.

Giving an artificial financial value to a non-financial benefit in order to justify some proposed expenditure would be a deception and could even be fraudulent, which is a serious criminal offence. Yet this is what many organizations not only encourage but pressurize staff into doing. Stephen Jenner makes this point very powerfully in his publication *Realising Benefits from Government ICT Investment* (Academic Publishing International, 2009).

A benefit should only be expressed in financial terms if it represents a real flow of money, either more money coming in or less money going out. Consider a team of people who improved their productivity and, as a consequence, produced 20% more widgets per week. Ignoring the cost of materials, can we give this a financial value? No. The financial value only comes with 'increased sales' when the widgets are sold. Surely the car industry learned this to its cost during the latter part of 2008, when it had great difficulty selling new cars and didn't know where to put all that it was producing.

What about the need to compare and choose between options? In our personal lives most of us are doing this all the time without tortuously putting financial values on benefits. How many families, when choosing between a new family car, an exotic family holiday or refurbishment of the kitchen try to compute net present values (NPVs), or use some other financial indicator, to make their decision? Instead, they are likely to involve the stakeholders – spouse, children, and possibly other relatives – and consider a whole range of factors, particularly costs and benefits (mainly non-financial).

If all investments could be analysed by just considering financials so that deciding between alternatives was reduced to a comparison of NPVs then most senior managers would be redundant. Most decision making involves weighing up the non-financials. Three helpful indicators which can be applied to non-financial benefits are:

- Business impact category
- Economic value
- Mapping score.

The most frequently used business impact category is the Cranfield Grid which can be applied to benefits to check for balance and alignment, and which also gives a good indication of relative importance (see Table 7.2).

Economic value is a monetary value assigned to a benefit. Its value is often computed by considering consequential effects – for example, the economic value associated with reduced crime might be calculated from:

- Lower NHS costs
- Lower insurance premiums for the public
- Reduced Crown Prosecution Service costs.

Since financial value and economic value are both monetary, it is important to maintain the distinction between them and not just add them together. The former represents real money while the latter is a pseudo-financial value computed from potential consequential improvements, often for stakeholders well removed from the organization making the investment.

If these consequential improvements are within the programme then they should be properly mapped and analysed like any other programme benefit, and the need for an economic value for a non-financial benefit largely disappears. However, if these consequential improvements sit outside the programme, as they usually do, then it is unlikely that anyone is managing the chain of activities to deliver them, raising serious concerns as to the likelihood of their achievement and casting doubts on the relevance of the economic value.

In the context of economic values, the Home Office website gives the average economic costs to be used for a death or for the emotional and physical impact on victims from sexual offences. How these economic values are computed will dictate how useful they are.

The third indicator of relative value is the mapping score provided from the maps by applying weightings to the paths. Calculation of this score is described in detail in sections 6.3 and 12.3. The score gives the relative contribution of the benefit to the ultimate goal.

11 Roles and responsibilities

11.1 ACCOUNTABILITY FOR BENEFIT REALIZATION

Since the primary purpose of any change activity should be to realize benefits, the person sponsoring the activity should carry the ultimate accountability for the realization of benefits. This is entirely consistent with OGC thinking, which recognizes the prime accountability of the SRO, who is a member of the sponsoring group, as being the realization of benefits. This works best when the SRO is a senior manager from the stakeholder group likely to experience the biggest proportion of the benefits.

For large changes many activities will need to be undertaken to achieve the benefits and these benefits may be realized in many different parts of the organization. Since SROs are normally very part time in their SRO role, their responsibility for benefit realization will need to be shared with or devolved to other players, including the:

- Programme board
- Programme manager
- Project board
- Project manager
- Business change managers
- Benefit owners.

The SROs will, however, retain their accountability for the realization of the benefits.

For a whole organization, accountability for optimized benefit realization rests with the portfolio board, which might be the executive board or senior management group. Where they exist, other roles which contribute to the realization of benefits include:

- Benefit facilitator
- Measure monitor
- Portfolio management office (PMO)
- Programme management office
- Project management office.

These roles, and the structures relating them together, will be considered in the following sections.

11.2 PORTFOLIO MANAGEMENT

Portfolio management is the oversight of an organization's investment in change, principally its programmes and projects. Its primary objectives are:

- To maximize the benefits realized from investment in change
- To help deliver the organization's vision and goals as cost-effectively as possible.

This will involve creating and maintaining the best possible portfolio of projects and programmes, and stimulating an environment in which they will thrive and deliver the highest possible returns for the business.

This is best achieved with a senior-level portfolio board supported by an efficient and effective portfolio office. The portfolio board should comprise a representative set of senior managers, often directors, from across the organization. Where practical, many, if not all, of the SROs should sit on this board (see MSP section 4.5).

Many organizations have such a board, though often with alternative names including: Steering Group, Sponsoring Group, Business Change

Board and Change Management Executive. Sometimes this board has a narrow focus, such as only overseeing IT projects. This is likely to lead to an unbalanced management of change and may not secure sufficient commitment from the business community within the organization. Wherever possible this board should be looking at the full range of investments in change and not a subset defined by investment type.

However, it is recognized that very large organizations may need more than one portfolio board, but where this is required it should be separated by business function rather than by type of change. There may still need to be an umbrella board to ensure cohesion and coordination across the organization.

Specific responsibilities of the portfolio board should include:

- Ensuring that the organization's mission, objectives and values are defined and clearly communicated so that the environment in which the portfolio sits is well understood.
- Encouraging an innovative culture where creative new ideas for change are spotted and promoted.
- Defining the portfolio balance appropriate for the organization, perhaps using the Cranfield Grid.
- Ensuring that there is a common approach to BRM to ensure consistency of comparisons both for initial selection and ongoing monitoring of investments in the portfolio. Ideally, the organization's methodology for programme and project management should be integrated around BRM. Where it exists, this may well fall within the remit of the organization's centre of excellence.
- Regular and active monitoring of the portfolio to ensure that only the most suitable investments are added to the portfolio and that programmes and projects are removed from the portfolio if they are not performing, or where priorities have changed.

Programmes and projects therefore depend on the portfolio board for their very existence and the managers of the programmes, and any projects which are not part of a programme, effectively report in to the portfolio board.

A more detailed consideration of portfolio management is given in Chapter 15.

11.3 PROGRAMME MANAGEMENT

A common structure for a programme is outlined in Figure 11.1.

A programme board, comprising senior representatives of the major stakeholders, will steer and support the programme through the auspices of the programme manager, who would normally be an ex-officio member of the programme board. This board would normally be chaired by the SRO. Extremely large programmes may require a programme director in addition to a programme manager.

In addition to their daily job, an SRO is frequently the SRO of several programmes and, as a result, can only act in a very part-time capacity (but normally no less than half a day per month). In view of the part-time nature of the SRO role, the manager of a programme of any size or significance would normally be full-time.

Roles and responsibilities | 75

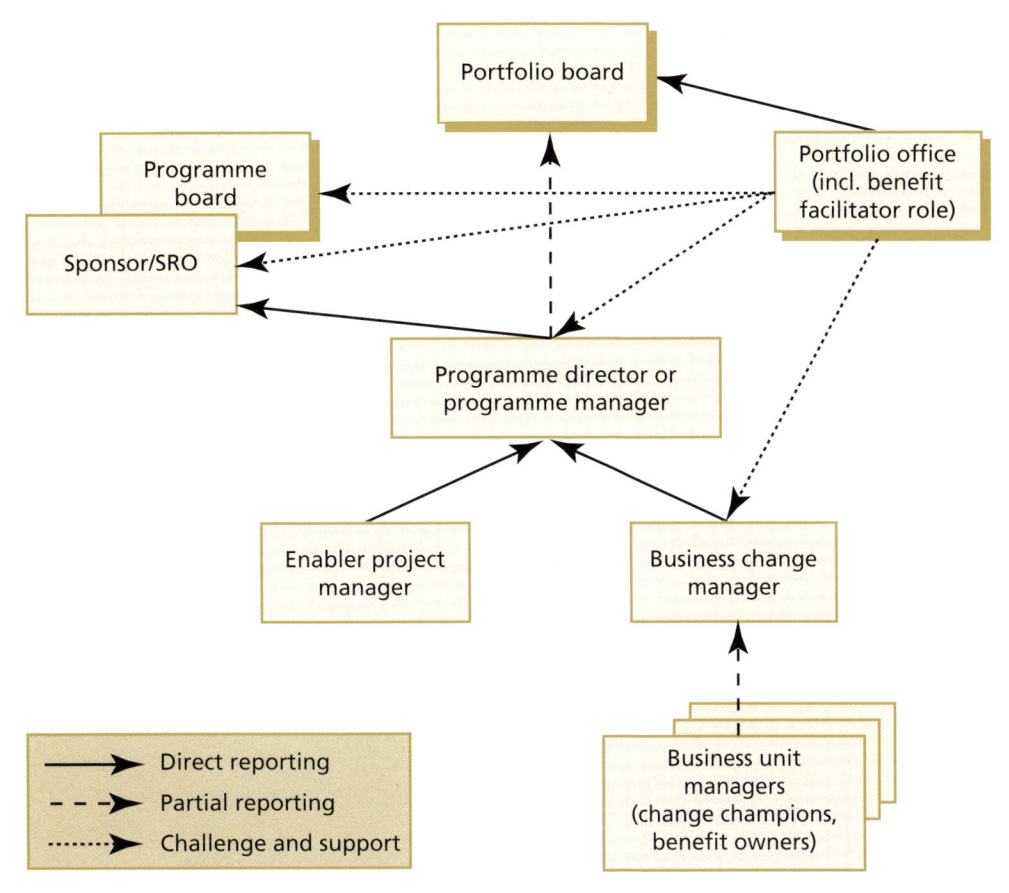

Figure 11.1 Typical programme structure

The programme manager is therefore acting on behalf of the SRO to ensure that the changes are designed and implemented appropriately and that the planned benefits are actually realized. Specific responsibilities include:

- Ensuring that there is a clear end goal, expressed as a vision or set of specific objectives and supported by a set of benefits
- The determination of the required changes, perhaps with ranked options
- The development of the blueprint – a picture of the future business state needed to ensure that the vision, objectives and benefits are achieved
- The specification of the detailed parts of the blueprint – enablers and business changes
- The building/acquisition of the enablers
- The implementation of the enablers and business changes and the transition into business as usual
- The realization of the benefits
- Establishing, within the business community, a benefit tracking and reporting mechanism.

To exercise this responsibility the programme manager will be supported by one or more project managers, each responsible for the acquisition and implementation of one or more enablers, and a business change manager, responsible for coordinating and overseeing the business change. Much of the required business change is likely to occur within a large number of different business units. So, to ensure a smooth and effective management of change, the business change manager may need to recruit, from within each business unit, a change champion.

A change champion will usually have a full-time job with little spare capacity. Therefore, their role will be that of an ambassador or evangelist, and not managerial.

For larger programmes the business change manager will often be a full-time role, coordinating, influencing and supporting change across a number of organizational units – often across the whole organization and, sometimes, outside of it too. For independent projects and smaller programmes the role of the business change manager may be incorporated into that of the programme or project manager.

If the business change manager is supporting the programme manager they should report directly to the programme manager, as indicated in Figure 11.1. This way the accountability for the success of the programme lies with a single full-time person, the programme manager, on behalf of the SRO. It also means that for a single programme the SRO only has one person reporting to them.

Some programme structures have the business change manager at the same level as the programme manager, both reporting to the SRO. In most situations, for the reasons outlined in the previous paragraph, there should be a single line of accountability (as in Figure 11.1). However, if the breadth of the change goes well beyond the sphere of influence of the programme manager but within the influence of the SRO then a direct line of reporting from the business change manager to the SRO may be helpful. MSP allows either line of reporting, although has a preference for the dual reporting to the SRO.

During the course of the programme the programme manager, in conjunction with the business change manager, will need to identify benefit owners for the benefits – where a benefit owner is the person responsible for the realization of a particular benefit. Most benefit owners will sit within the business community and, ideally, will have a personal interest in their benefit being realized. Their role will continue beyond the life of the programme.

Additional support for the programme comes from the programme office, if one exists. There is a clear distinction between the portfolio office, which is looking across the whole portfolio of programmes and projects in support of the portfolio board, and the programme office, which serves a single programme and is part of the programme structure. Both offices are sometimes referred to as management offices (PMOs) and sometimes as support offices (PSOs).

The above programme-related roles all come into existence within the life of a programme and will cease, except for benefit owners, once the programme is closed. If programme closure is delayed until all benefits have been realized, then the role of the benefit owners would also cease on programme closure. However, this deferred closure would generally be considered impractical.

Another role that supports the programme manager but which exists before the programme comes into being is that of benefit facilitator. This role both challenges and supports those programme roles which are responsible for the realization of benefits – the SRO, programme manager, business change manager and benefit owners. It has been successfully implemented by many organizations over the past 20 years, often becoming the centre of excellence for BRM, and is ideally located within the portfolio management office.

This role is recommended in MSP, where it is referred to as the benefit realization manager. There is a real risk, however, that if the role is called benefit realization manager then those responsible for benefits (SRO, programme manager, business change manager and benefit owners) may abdicate their responsibility to the benefit realization manager.

Another organizational structure which has been employed, to good effect, in some large government programmes is illustrated in Figure 11.2.

11.4 PROJECT MANAGEMENT

Project management takes two forms, one where the project is part of a programme and one where the project stands on its own.

When a project is part of a programme it is usually focused on the delivery and implementation of one or more enablers and is often referred to as an enabler project. The enabler project managers will report in to the programme manager and the related management of business change and realization of benefits will probably be managed at programme level. This allows the project manager to focus on what they should be good at – delivering the enabler on time, within budget and to the required quality.

In this situation the project may not need its own project board or business case but can just come under the auspices of the programme.

In contrast, a standalone project should report directly to a portfolio board and include responsibility for managing or overseeing the required business changes and the realization of the benefits. It will need its own business case and project board and may require the help of a project support office.

There will be many parallels between a standalone project and a programme. Therefore, the process and many of the techniques described in Part 2 would also be applicable to a standalone project.

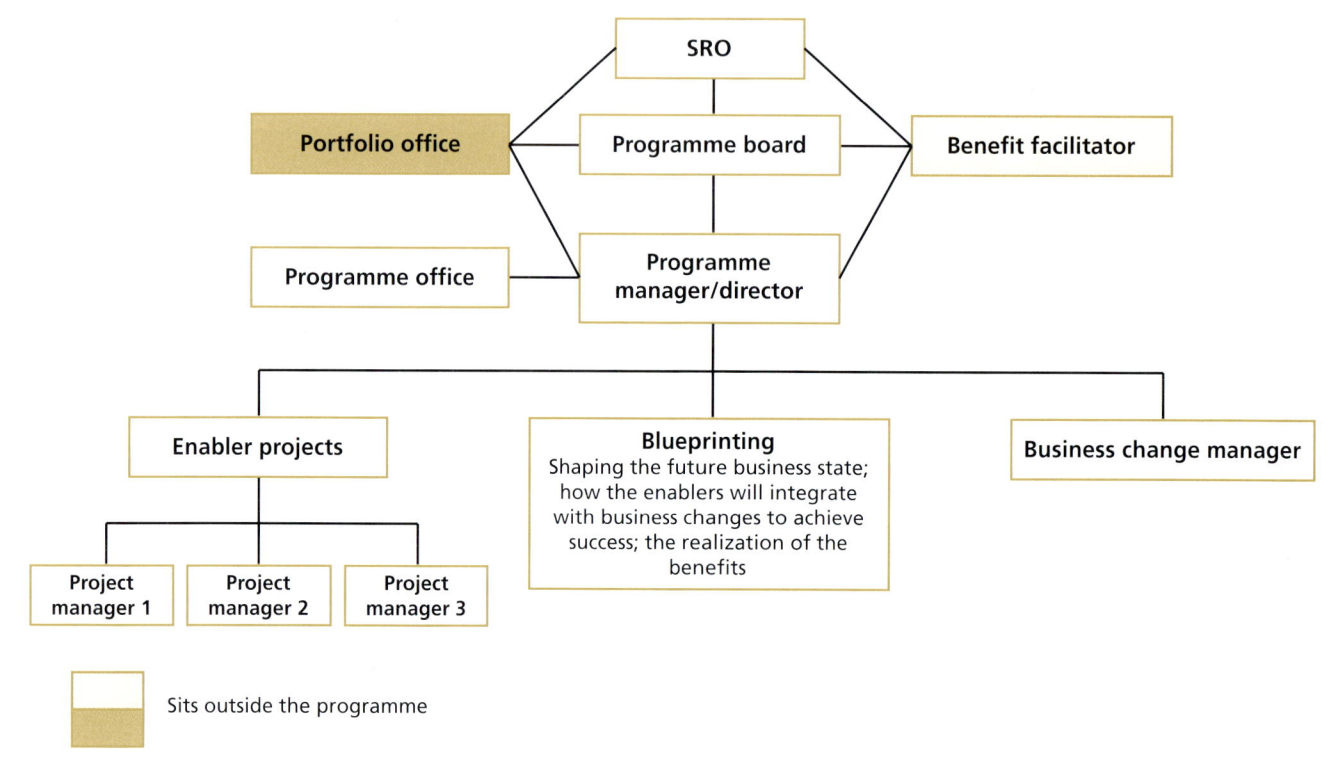

Figure 11.2 Alternative organizational structure (for large programmes)

12 Mapping

12.1 THE IMPORTANCE OF MAPPING

Many organizations determine a solution or identify some enablers and then seek benefits to justify the cost. Effective change starts by establishing the destination, at least in approximate terms, and then determines the route to get there. Creating this route will identify and define the required enablers and changes.

A fundamental part of the BRM process is the creation of route maps defining the path from where we are now (the 'as is') to where we want to be (the 'to be'). For this we need to understand the starting point and then work with the business community – the relevant stakeholders – to articulate the destination, which may be expressed as a vision statement or a set of objectives. The route then needs to be mapped, which is normally done working back from the destination.

Even when a destination is articulated, instead of working back from this to determine the required changes, organizations often jump to a solution (which may have already been determined for them). Figure 12.1 illustrates this common situation, where the objectives on the right define the destination or end goal, and the enablers on the left are thought to define the solution. Ideally, we would start on the right-hand side and then work right to left to determine the required solution. However, it may be that the solution has already been determined by:

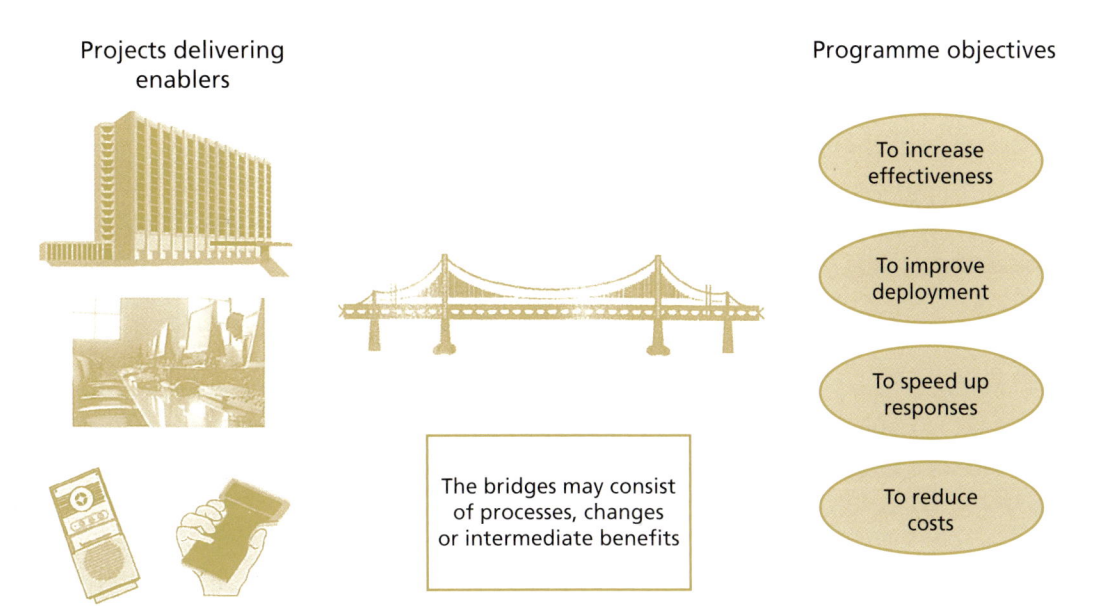

Figure 12.1 Bridging the abyss

- A higher-level authority (e.g. the corporate board has decided that the whole global organization is to implement SAP)
- A political decision
- Someone's whim
- A previous non-BRM process.

Even when the solution (the left-hand side of Figure 12.1) is a given, it is still essential to understand how the specified enablers are going to deliver the objectives. Without this information the outcome is left to chance, which is totally irresponsible. It is amazing, then, that so many business cases predominantly focus on the ROI or NPV calculation giving little attention to the realism of the logic as to how the benefits will be delivered.

If the business case does not contain a very clear description of how the enablers will deliver the defined objectives and benefits, it should be rejected no matter how good the ROI or NPV appears to be. This would significantly reduce the large amount of wasted investment each year – programmes and projects which yield little or no benefits. (OGC estimates that 30–40% of systems that support business change deliver no benefits whatsoever.)

A fundamental part of BRM is the development of one or more maps which define the route from the 'as is' to the 'to be', or the bridge between planned or imposed enablers and desired outcomes.

12.2 TYPES OF MAP

Many approaches to benefit realization now recognize the need for some kind of mapping. The central thread of the following chapters is based on an approach which has been extensively tested in a variety of environments and underpins the ideas in MSP. It is a powerful and comprehensive process for determining requirements – for both enablers and business changes – and so for scoping the change.

The mapping is built up in three stages:

1. Creation of a **strategy map** of linked objectives. The objectives are determined from the vision, if one exists, or from the drivers for change. These usually arise from a combination of fixing problems and exploiting opportunities. Once created, the strategy map is used to determine the objectives that define the boundary of the potential change initiative, generally referred to as the bounding objectives. The change initiative is usually a programme, though it may be a standalone project. This stage normally results in two, three or occasionally four bounding objectives and is a powerful approach for realistically scoping the potential programme.

2. For each bounding objective a **benefits map** is created. This starts by identifying a set of end benefits which are mutually independent but together equate to the bounding objective (that is, if they are fully achieved then the objective would be fully achieved). Once there is confidence in the end benefits, feeder benefits are determined. This process continues working right to left until the whole map is complete. When first created the benefits map is a structured wish list, carefully determined, starting with a bounding objective and then applying a combination of logic and understanding of the business. It is generally cleaner, and improves later communication, if a separate map is created for each bounding objective. However, if two objectives are likely to require a large proportion of similar feeder benefits, it may work better if both are included in the same map.

3. **The BDM.** Once a benefits map has been developed, refined and agreed it can be transformed into a BDM by identifying, and adding to the map, the enablers and business changes needed to deliver the benefits. This process works left to right through the benefits map, asking for each benefit being considered what needs to change to deliver it. This change is a mix of enablers and business changes which combine with any feeder benefits to deliver the new benefit.

Creating these maps is a detailed and challenging process, requiring well-facilitated stakeholder engagement, but it is the very heart of the change process and fundamental to effective benefit realization. In fact, the mapping process should help to define and populate many of the required programme and project documents as indicated in Figure 12.2.

The maps themselves are useful for:

- Identifying a comprehensive set of benefits
- Determining required enablers and business changes

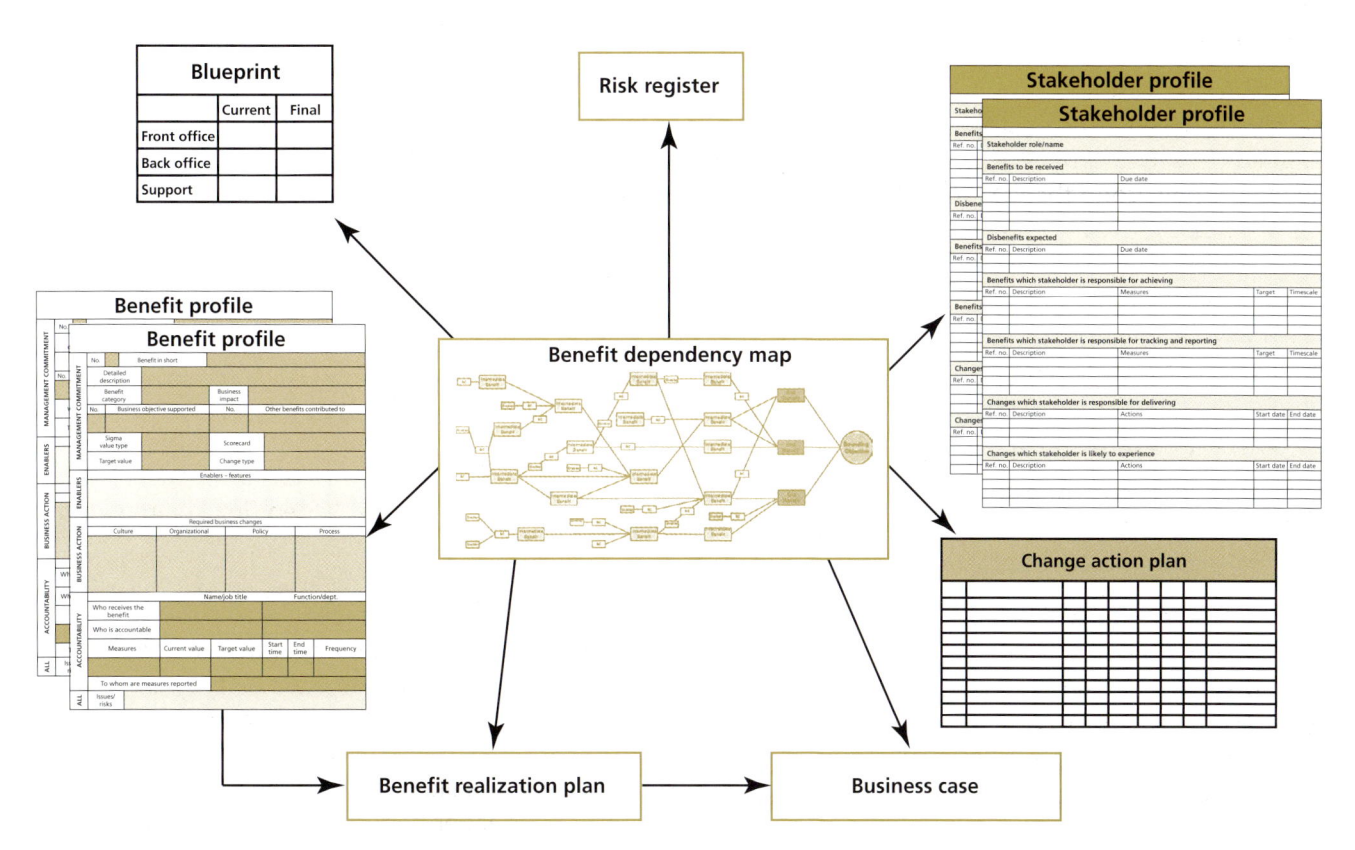

Figure 12.2 The centrality of the BDM

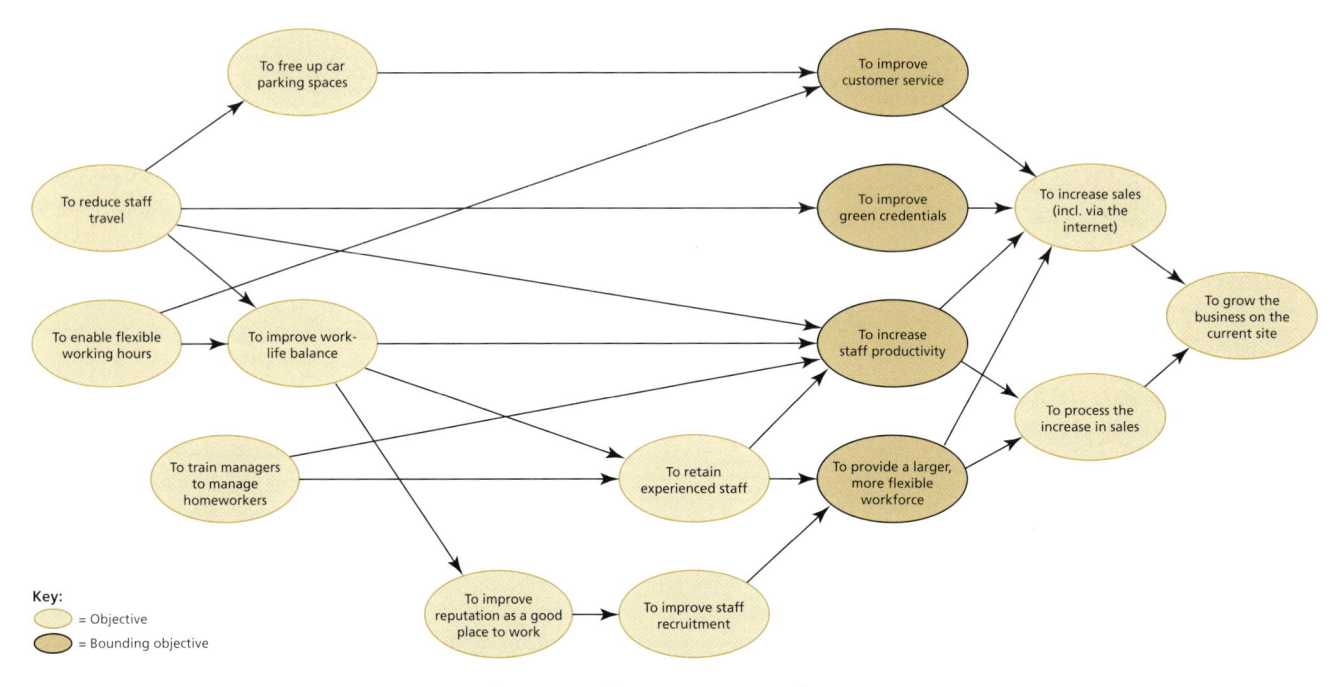

Part 3: Elaboration of key techniques and responsibilities

Figure 12.3 Strategy map to consider homeworking to grow a business on its current site

- Assessing the impact of unexpected changes – internal and external
- Aiding prioritization
- Sequencing implementation
- Communicating expectations
- Tracking benefits
- Avoiding double counting of benefits
- Attributing benefits to their source
- Maximizing benefit realization.

Examples of the three types of map, in a related set, are illustrated in Figure 12.3. They are based on a company exploring homeworking as a means of growing its business on its existing site. Expansion of the facilities on the existing site was not an option.

From the development of this strategy map the company considered that the darker-shaded objectives would provide a meaningful bounding set for the potential programme. For each of these bounding objectives, more detailed benefits maps were developed.

The benefits map for the objective 'to increase staff productivity' is shown in Figure 12.4.

The development of each benefits map starts with a bounding objective and works right to left, first determining a set of end benefits (darker shading) that are the equivalent of the objective. The test for these is that they are:

- Collectively sufficient – equivalent to the objective
- Individually necessary
- Mutually independent.

Mapping | **83**

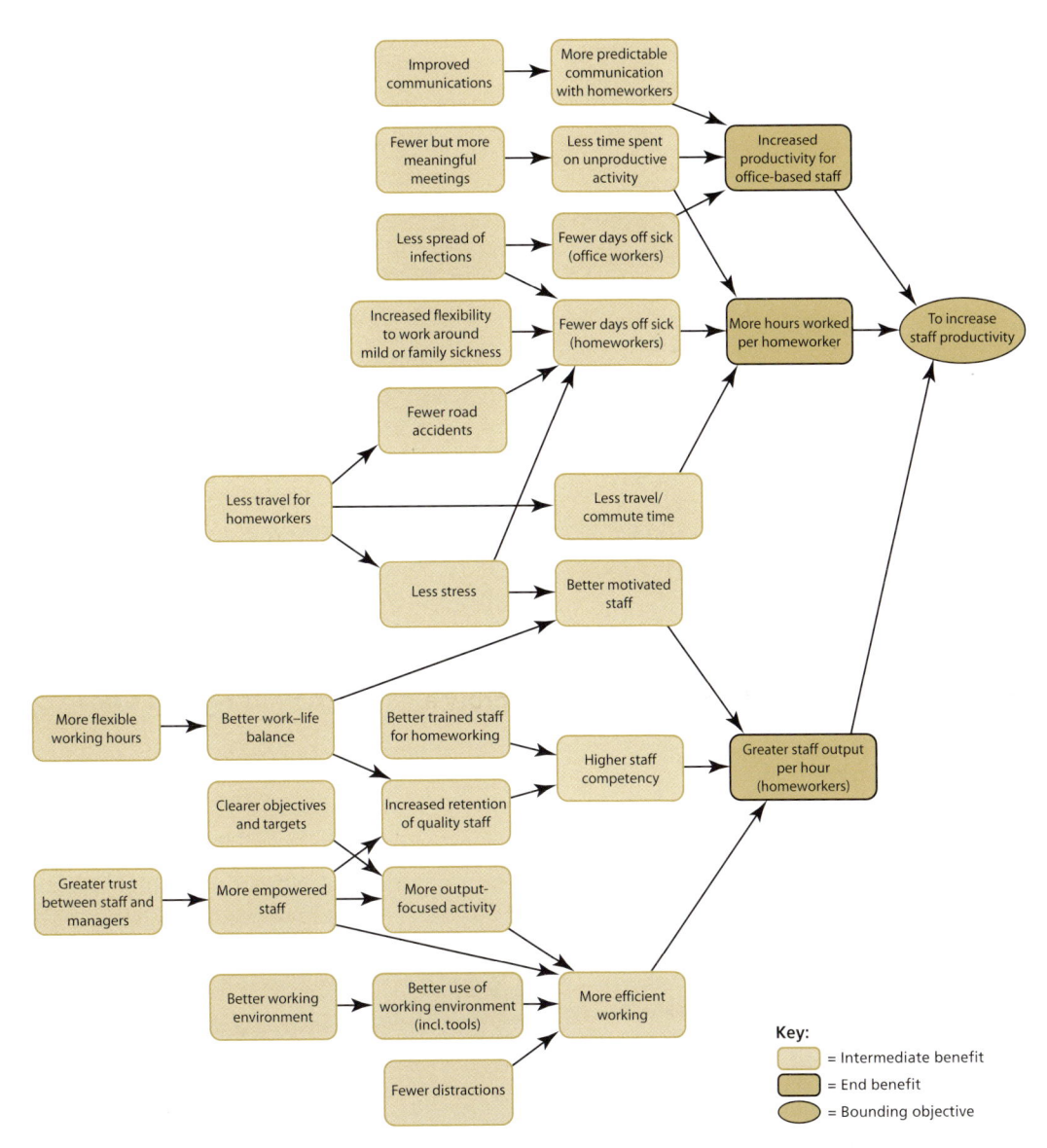

Figure 12.4 Benefits map for the objective 'to increase staff productivity'

Once the end benefits are agreed the feeder benefits are determined, progressively working right to left. These feeder benefits can be regarded as the improvements necessary to delivery the benefit, and are generally referred to as intermediate benefits (lighter shading).

All these benefits are determined, in the sequence described above, through the application of logic to an understanding of the business/operational environment. At this stage infeasibility to deliver a benefit because of cost, risk or resource requirements is not a consideration, so the resulting map is just a set of aspirations – but carefully constructed so that their fulfilment would ensure the complete achievement of the objective.

The next stage of the process is to work through the map from left to right identifying the changes (enablers and business changes) that need to be implemented in order to deliver each of the benefits. In this example, the result is the map shown in Figure 12.5 (a BDM), where the lightest shaded boxes are enablers and the unshaded boxes are business changes.

12.3 WEIGHTING THE PATHS OF THE MAPS

In order to prioritize investment and activity the paths of these maps can be weighted. This would be undertaken working progressively right to left, applying percentage weightings to the paths. The percentage describes the relative importance of the contribution from the entity on its left to the entity on its right, taking account of intrinsic importance and room for improvement. The percentage distribution may be used as an indicator of the degree of emphasis or focus (even budget) to be invested to achieve the required entity – objective or benefit.

Once the weighting process is complete a score can be computed for each benefit by giving an initial score (usually a large round number like 1,000) to the bounding objective, and then performing the necessary arithmetic, working right to left, to calculate the scores for the other entities. This

Example

A large public-sector organization, intent on a significant cross-organizational transformation, invested heavily in lean thinking. It identified several hundred improvement opportunities, far more than it had the resources to undertake. It had difficulty knowing which improvements to undertake and when, and in particular what was required to achieve the organization's strategy.

It subsequently applied BRM, creating a set of eight BDMs tied back into a high-level strategy map, ensuring that the benefits would contribute to the organization's strategy. The previously identified improvement opportunities appeared in the BDMs, alongside some newly identified change requirements.

Each of the BDMs was then weighted by stakeholders relevant to its theme and the top team weighted the high-level strategy map. A notional score of 10,000 was then given to the objective furthest to the right on the strategy map, and the application of simple arithmetic produced scores for each of the improvement opportunities. Some improvements had scores as low as 1, 2 and 3 while others had scores of 150, 200, 330 etc. This enabled the organization to prioritize the improvements, confident of their contribution to the strategy and the value they would generate.

scoring process can be undertaken for a single map or for the complete set of maps for a programme. In the latter case the initial score would be entered at the right-hand end of the strategy map and the calculation could then be automatically cascaded down through the maps. Figure 12.6 illustrates how this cascade works for a strategy map to a benefits map for one of the three bounding objectives.

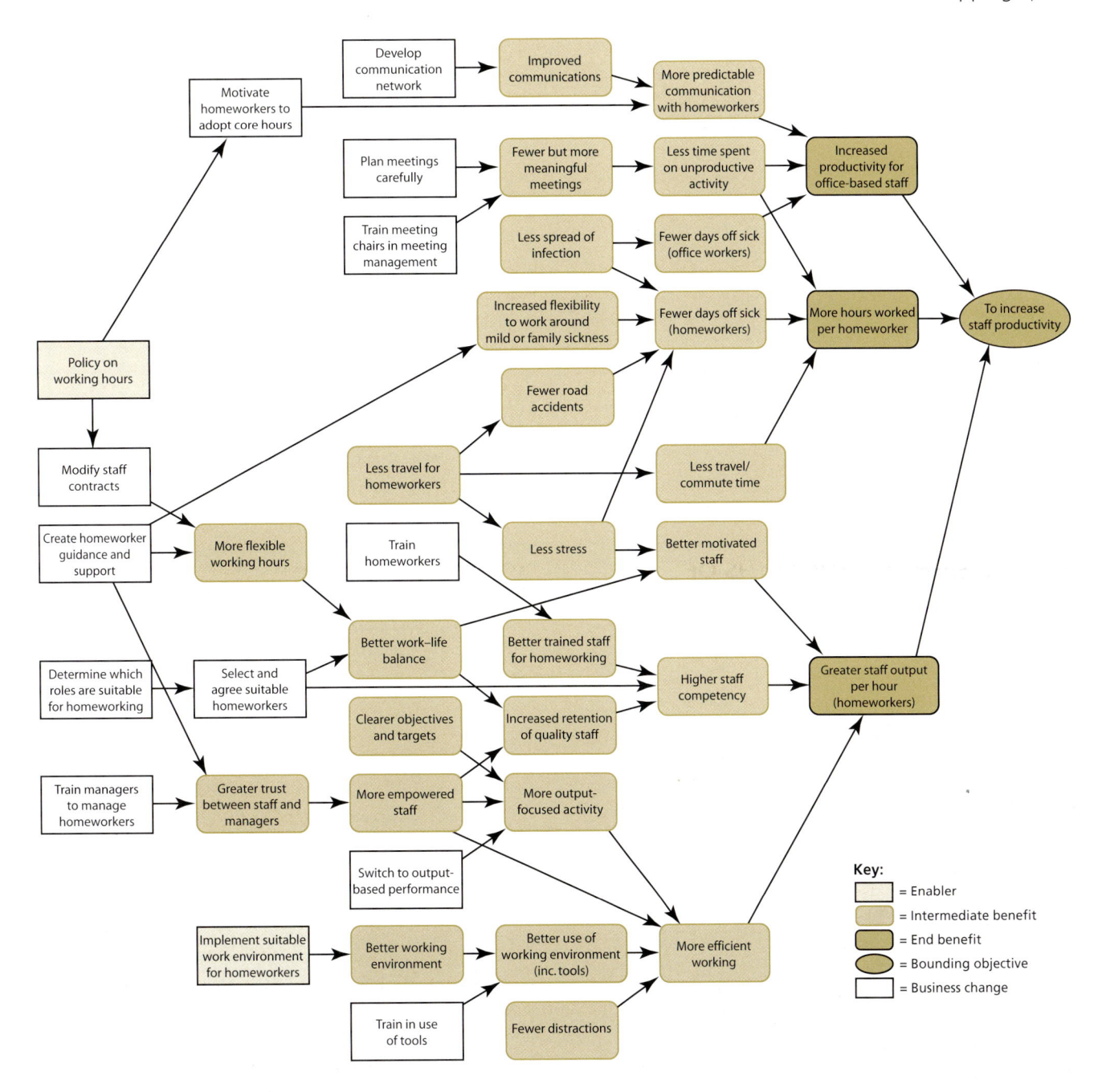

Figure 12.5 A BDM for the objective 'to increase overall staff productivity'

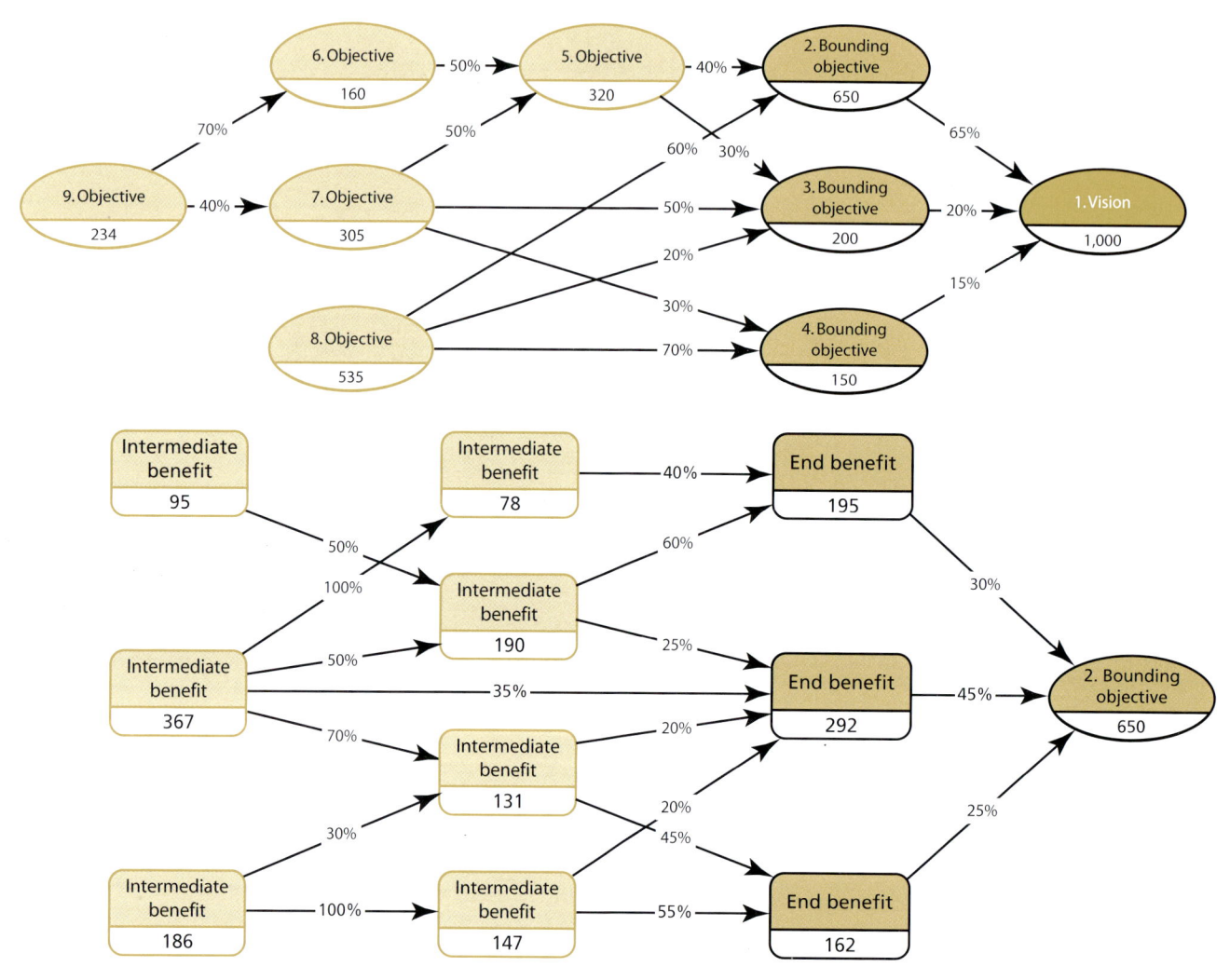

Figure 12.6 Linked weighted generic maps for objectives and benefits

In Figure 12.6 the scores of the left-hand side benefits are very different to each other. This immediately gives guidance as to where to focus energies on the left-hand side and can therefore aid the prioritization process.

Although this technique is extremely useful it is only a broad guide. It should be used with caution and not on its own. It is not rigorous science and it depends on the quality of the underlying map and the consistency with which the percentages are determined. Both need to be undertaken in a workshop with relevant stakeholders.

In order to apply this technique in this way, it is important to first ensure that if an enabler and a business change are both required in order to improve the value of a benefit, then they are linked in sequence; if either on its own can result in an improvement in the benefit then they should be linked in parallel. The two options are illustrated in Figure 12.7.

In option (a) it is best to treat the combination of enabler-business change as a single entity. So, for the purpose of calculating meaningful map scores, you can either give the link from the enabler to the business change a weight of 0% or give it 100% provided the weight on the link between the business change and the benefit is reduced to 50% of what it otherwise would be.

If the paths in the strategy map and the related BDMs are all weighted, and a notional score is given to the right-hand side of the strategy map, say 10,000, then scores can be computed for all the entities in all the maps by arithmetically applying the percentage weightings. Figure 12.8 is an example of how this could be applied to an NHS programme for improving operating theatre utilization.

If a benefits map is weighted before enablers and changes are added, then the further to the left you go the less stringent you need to be on the sufficiency criterion (i.e. weights adding to 100%), as any shortfall or gap may be filled by an enabler or a change.

If a budget for the programme exists, this value can be applied to the strategy map instead of the notional score. This then gives each enabler and business change its benchmark value, which can then be compared to its likely cost. If an enabler comes out with a benchmark value of £25,000 but is only likely to cost £5,000 it becomes a 'no brainer' and is a clear candidate for the programme plan. Alternatively, if its cost is £100,000 it is almost certainly not a candidate for the programme plan – although before a decision to reject it is made, the full implications of not delivering the enabler should be examined.

Key:
- = Enabler
- = Business change
- = Benefit

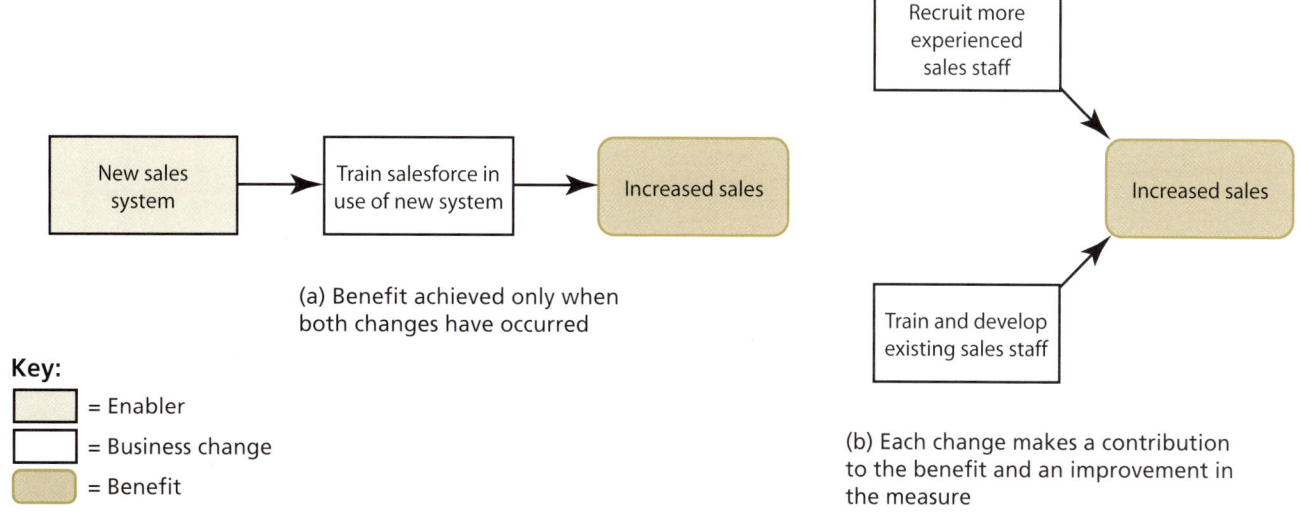

(a) Benefit achieved only when both changes have occurred

(b) Each change makes a contribution to the benefit and an improvement in the measure

Figure 12.7 Change to benefit relationships

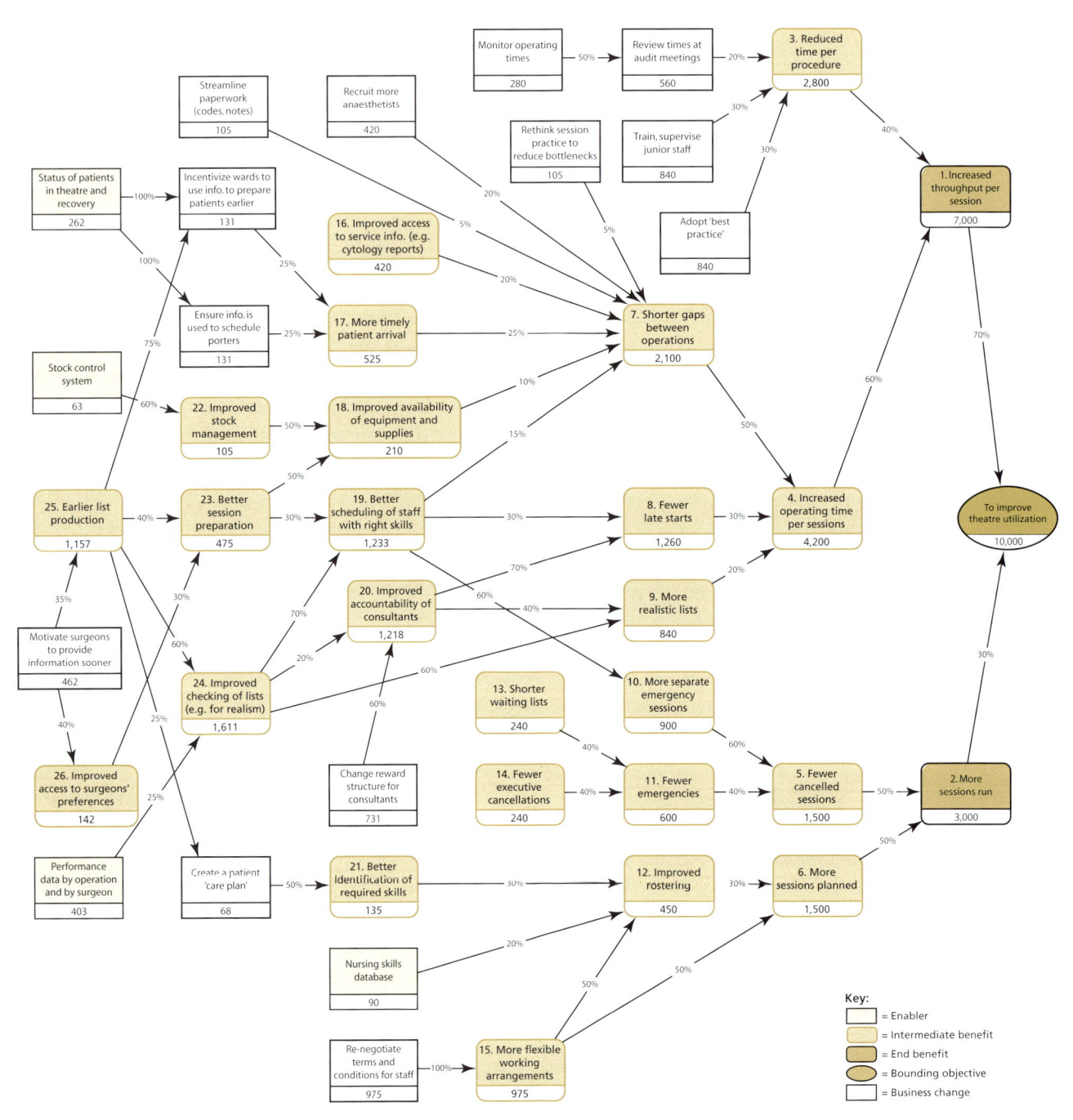

Part 3: Elaboration of key techniques and responsibilities

Figure 12.8 Weighted and scored BDM for improving theatre utilization

13 Measuring

13.1 THE PURPOSE OF MEASURING

The primary purpose of measurement should be to inform decision making and drive action. Consider the dashboard of a motor vehicle – it displays a set of measurements primarily to enable the driver to drive the vehicle effectively and safely – that is, to influence action. These measurements would normally also provide information to enable the driver to monitor progress. Although part of monitoring progress is to provide reassurance and comfort, a big part is also to influence action. A driver may change their route or drive faster if they are behind schedule, but the speedometer may encourage the desired behaviour of staying within speed limits.

In summary, the objectives for measurement are:

- To monitor progress over time
- To inform decision making and drive action
- To encourage desired behaviours.

Generally, measurement will inform immediate decision making, leading to early, often remedial, action. But, by monitoring progress, lessons may be learned which could influence future decision making.

13.2 DEFINITIONS AND MEASURE ATTRIBUTES

In section 10.1 a measure was defined as 'the entity whose value is reported regularly to demonstrate the realization of the benefit'. It is normally computed from a combination of metrics (the raw data), often collected automatically by the organization.

The simplest computation is where the measure equals the metric. Most measures will be more sophisticated than this – for example, if the metric is the recorded detail of calls to a call centre, many meaningful measures are possible from the same set of metrics, including the average response time, the median response time and the longest response time.

The measure is the entity whose value is to be reported (for example, 'total monthly sales value') – it is not the value itself (for example, £300,000), the predicted improvement (for example, +30%), the means of measurement or reporting (for example, quarterly financial review), nor the benefit (for example, more sales). This measure will be computed from the set of metrics – the values of the individual sales. Other measures can be computed from this same set of metrics, such as the percentage of sales which are less than £20,000 or the average sales value for a specific product. By combining with other metrics we can create combination measures such as the average annual sales per employee.

Some related terms include:

- Baseline – **a line or set of values used as a base or starting point**
- Target or predicted value – **the value predicted for a measure as a consequence of the proposed change**
- Benchmark – **an industry standard for a particular measure, often used to determine a target**.

The term 'predicted value' may be preferable to 'target' to avoid the negative connotations associated with the word 'target'.

13.3 MEASURE ATTRIBUTES AND CATEGORIES

Measures have many important attributes or related characteristics. Some relate only to the measure, irrespective of the related benefit. These include:

- Unit of measure
- The combination of metrics which define the measure (the formula)
- Frequency of measurement and reporting
- Method of measurement
- Baseline value, if available
- Measure category (e.g. value type)

- Predicted value, where appropriate (see Figures 10.1 and 13.1)
- Improvement timescale – T1 to T3 for M1, and T2 to T4 for M2 (see Figure 6.4)
- Measure monitor – person responsible for monitoring the measure
- Beneficiary of the expected improvement.

Other attributes relate to the specific benefit-measure relationship, and these include:

- Benefit-measure contribution – this is the predicted contribution to the measure expected from the particular benefit: MV1 to MV2 for Benefit 1, and MV2 to MV3 for Benefit 2 in Figure 13.1
- Improvement timescale – T1 to T2 for Benefit 1, T2 to T3 for Benefit 2 (see Figure 13.1)

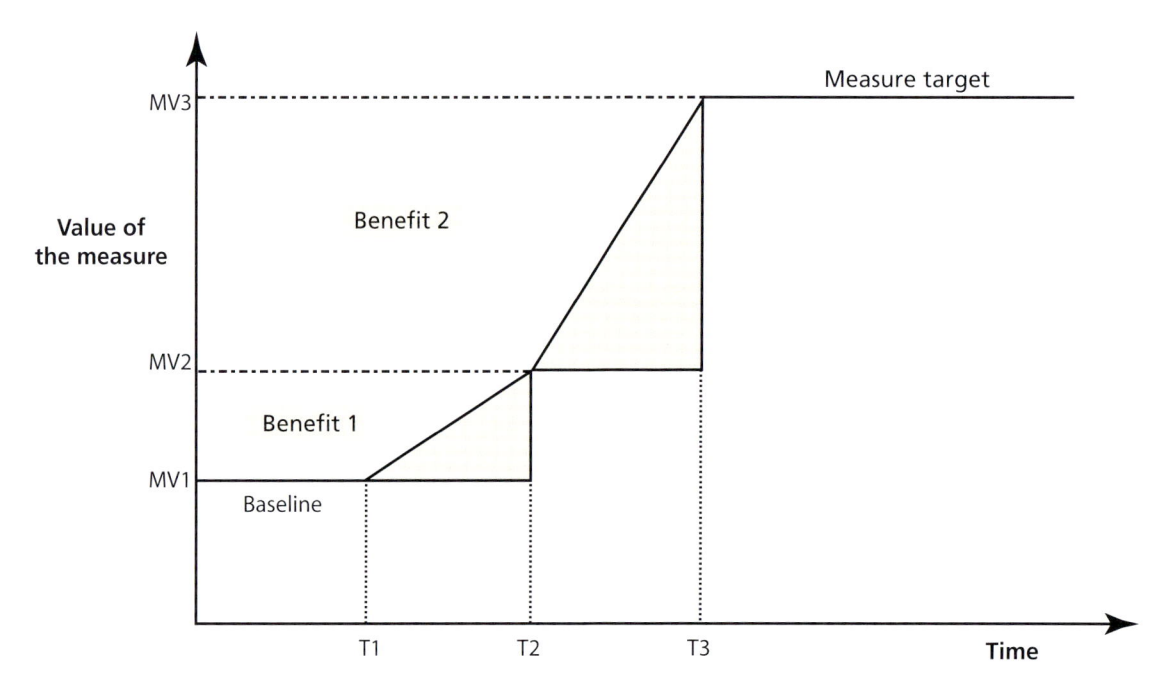

Figure 13.1 Benefit-measure contributions

- Owner or accountable person – the person accountable for the improvement in the measure related to the particular benefit, usually the benefit owner.

If in Figure 13.1 Benefit 1 is expected from Programme A, and Benefit 2 from Programme B, then both programmes are contributing to the desired improvement in the measure, which itself may relate to a corporate goal and so may be a key performance indicator (KPI), a balanced scorecard category or a benefits bucket (a term used by some organizations to describe a corporate benefit to which many programmes may contribute). Attributing improvements in the measure of a particular programme is difficult, though it becomes easier if we can separate the improvement times (see Figure 13.1) and/or we are monitoring the achievement of all the feeder benefits.

13.4 CHARACTERISTICS OF GOOD MEASURES

A good measure:

- Motivates behaviour, which will contribute to success
- Meets the needs of relevant stakeholders
- Supports, or at least does not undermine, the vision or end goal.

Example

In 2004, the UK national press reported two situations where a young patient urgently needed an ambulance and suffered trauma because none was available. In each instance there was a queue of ambulances containing patients outside the local hospital's accident and emergency department (A&E) because the department was not ready to accept the patients. The ambulance service had no doubt transported their patients to the hospital fast enough to achieve their response time targets for getting patients to hospital quickly. A&E was achieving its targets for dealing with patients within a certain time by getting the ambulance crews to hang on to their patients until they were ready to deal with them. Both the ambulance service and A&E were meeting their targets, but this was definitely not benefiting the primary stakeholder – the patient.

This is a classic case of targets that do not relate to measures which are for the benefit of the primary stakeholder, in this case the patient. The measure should have been the time taken between the 999 call and commencement of appropriate hospital treatment. Had this more relevant, end-to-end measure been used, the outcomes may have been quite different.

The most appropriate measure is sometimes not chosen because:

- The measure would be difficult to monitor
- Targets would be more difficult to achieve
- The measure may span more than one department, or even more than one organization
- No one in the organization has the vision to realize that the proposed combination of individual targets will not achieve the overall target.

A serious danger is that those metrics which are easy to monitor will be chosen. Because it is so important that measurement encourages the desired behaviour, it is worth spending time, in consultation with the stakeholders, determining suitable measures, even though they may prove difficult to monitor.

> **Example**
> Within the NHS one metric which was being monitored was the number of cancellations of surgical operations. This metric did not distinguish between the reasons for the cancellation or whether the re-scheduled surgery was brought forward or put back. One NHS surgeon frequently brought forward patients' operations, to their delight. Each time this happened, it registered as a cancellation of the originally scheduled time, and the surgeon was eventually penalized for the rise in cancellations – which was a result of commitment and dedication.

Elaborating on the three general criteria listed at the start of this section, measures should be:

- Relevant – would change in value matter to stakeholders and encourage desired behaviour?
- In the appropriate format – would a ratio or percentage be more appropriate than an absolute value? Would a median or maximum be more appropriate than an average?
- Predictable – will it be reasonably easy for the relevant stakeholders to predict a realistic value for the potential improvement?
- Inexpensive to track – are the underlying metrics for the measure already captured by the organization or can they be captured by a proposed system?
- Incorruptible – could individuals take inappropriate action to massage the values?
- Timely – will reporting frequency be sufficient to observe trends without being onerous?

- Unambiguous – can results be displayed visually in such a way that all stakeholders can easily understand them?
- Consistent – will the metrics be collected in the same way, using the same criteria, for the foreseeable future?

More than one measure is often required to ensure that the right outcome is achieved, sometimes a pair of complementary or contrasting measures – for example, a caller to a call centre may, in general, want the length of the dialogue with the call handler to be as short as possible but without the call handler being impolite. Two complementary or contrasting measures are needed – one monitoring the length of the dialogue and the other the courtesy of the call handler.

13.5 CHOOSING WHICH BENEFITS TO MEASURE

Measuring benefits requires effort and money. As a result, there is a general reluctance to measure at all and, understandably, people are not keen to measure all the benefits that might be identified in a set of maps. A more practical option would be to just measure the so-called key benefits, particularly if some seem very difficult to measure. However, this is not a good strategy because:

- There are no meaningful criteria for choosing key benefits
- By not measuring all, or close to all, of the benefits, attributing success to the programme may be incredibly difficult
- By not measuring all, or close to all, of the benefits, it will be impossible to spot quickly those parts of a map which are not working and remedy the cause of the problem

- By not measuring all, or close to all the benefits, progress towards the end goal cannot be monitored.

Furthermore, the measurement load can often be shared between motivated stakeholders and so not be as onerous as it first appears.

Figure 13.2 shows a simplified version of a benefits map produced for an organization that had commissioned three programmes to help increase sales revenue. Business changes have been excluded from this version of the map in order to focus attention on benefit tracking and reporting. It is often helpful to present limited views of maps to aid communication and increase focus on the issue at hand.

Often benefits on the right-hand side of a map are open to influence from activities external to the programme (for example, from one of the other initiatives commissioned by the sales director), and sometimes external to the organization (for example, a competitor going out of business). Those on the left-hand side of the map, however, are usually more directly related to the programme. If movements through the map are monitored, their convergence on the end benefit should give confidence that the particular improvement in sales revenue is a consequence of the programme.

When considering benefit tracking we must not ignore the cost of measuring. Some benefits in this example may be considered difficult to measure. This often means that more elaboration is required (for example, what aspect of staff morale could be improved?) and/or the cost of measurement is high (for example, improved image).

At the other end of the spectrum, some benefits could be tracked at zero or low cost to the programme, because they are already being measured (for example, errors, productivity, overtime, new customers and sales revenue).

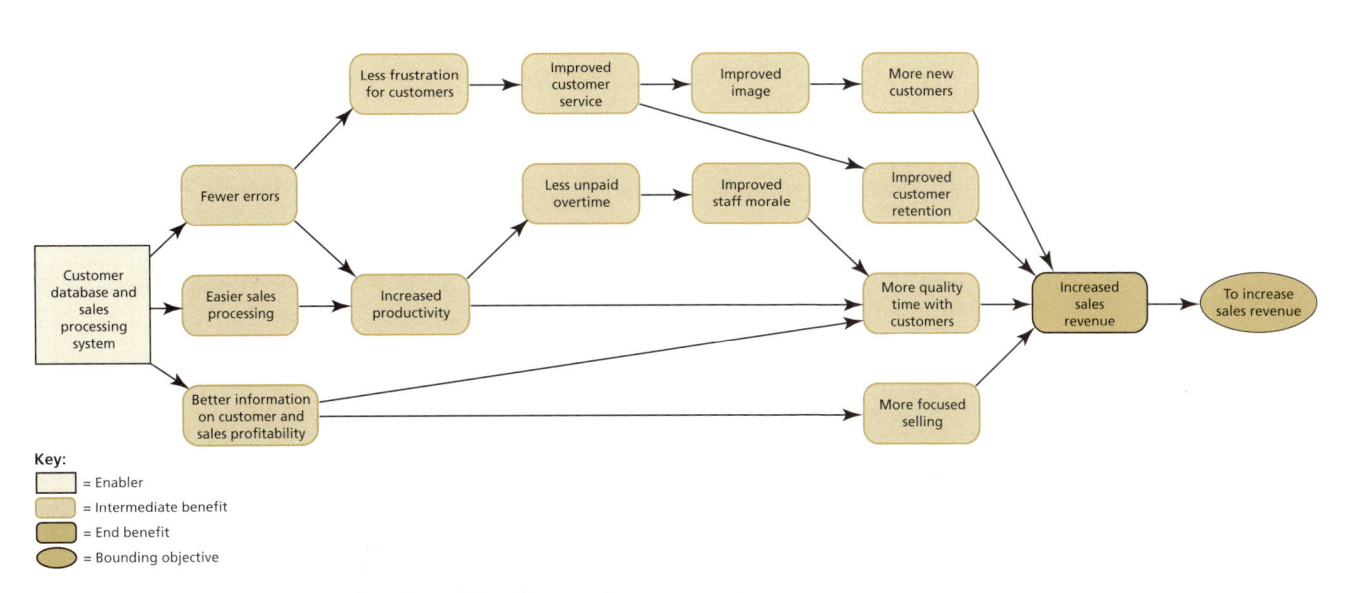

Figure 13.2 Benefits map for the objective 'to increase sales revenue'

Because measurement can be time-consuming and costly there is often pressure to measure only a few benefits – the key benefits. However sensible this seems, it can be a disastrous strategy. Looking at the benefits map in Figure 13.2, the key benefits, at least initially, are fewer errors, easier sales processing and better information on customers and sales profitability, since without these none of the other benefits will be achieved. Once these three are achieved, the key benefits become those immediately to their right, and so on.

Ultimately all benefits are key benefits. However, some may decide that the key benefit is 'increased sales revenue' because:

- It is the end benefit
- It is clearly of great interest to the sponsor (the sales director)
- It is the only financial benefit on the map
- It is easy to track because it was already being measured by the bank.

However, only tracking the end benefit is a waste of time because it would not reveal anything useful about the programme. We would not know whether any change in sales revenue was attributable to the programme, or which parts of the programme are working and which are not.

If possible all benefits should be tracked. If one or two are particularly difficult to measure, the best compromise would be to measure benefits either side of the difficult ones. This works best when there is only a single feed in and out of the 'difficult to measure' benefit, such as 'improved image' in Figure 13.2.

Although all benefits are key benefits and therefore should be tracked, some organizations will insist that only a subset of the benefits in a map should be measured. In this situation the best practice is to use the weighting and scoring process (described in section 12.3) to determine the best benefits to track – for example, from a map of 30 benefits, the 10 highest-scoring could be selected.

However many benefits are selected for tracking, it is important to engage the business community in measuring and, whenever possible, to share the measurement load between different stakeholders.

13.6 RESPONSIBILITIES

The responsibility for measurement must, ultimately, lie with the business – although the process may be started and established by the programme team and, after the programme is complete and the team has moved on, audited by the benefit facilitator.

This business responsibility may be shared by various stakeholders provided they are motivated to see the benefits realized – for example, in the benefits map illustrated in Figure 13.2:

- The sales processing manager would be interested in the three benefits: fewer errors, easier sales processing and increased productivity
- The customer relationship manager would be interested in the four benefits: fewer errors, less frustration for customers, improved customer service, and improved image
- The sales director would be interested in the five benefits: more new customers, improved customer retention, more quality time with customers, more focused selling and increased sales revenue
- The HR director may be interested in the three benefits: increased productivity, less unpaid overtime and improved staff morale.

If these interests are genuine it should be relatively easy to co-opt these stakeholders to measure and report the benefits in which they have an interest.

13.7 TRACKING AND REPORTING

The benefits map is a key tool in tracking and attributing benefits. It operates like a signalling map of train movements – as time passes, steady movement along the paths or tracks can be seen, with benefits lit up as targets are achieved (or missed), based on a colour convention such as blue, red, amber and green (BRAG).

When attributing benefits is difficult, as is the case with 'increased sales revenue' in the banking example (section 13.5, Figure 13.2), the benefits map is one of the best vehicles to provide confidence that the realization of the benefit, indicated by an improvement in its measure, is attributable to the programme.

Tracking and reporting the benefits may be done using a tabular format and/or using the map (examples are illustrated in Figures 13.3 and 13.4).

In Figure 13.3, the shading indicates which stakeholder is likely to receive the benefit and therefore which stakeholder may be persuaded to track and report the benefit.

In this instance the suggested reporting frequency is three monthly and all measures are tracked and reported each period, even though benefits on

Measure	Baseline value	Start period	End period	Target value	Period 1	Period 2	Period 3	Period 4
No. of errors per 100 sales	7.5	1	3	2.5	7	4	3	2.5
No. of written complaints per week	9	2	4	2	10	8	6	4
No. of phone complaints per week		2	4	5	25	21	15	9
Customer service rating (%)	55	3	8	80	55	60	70	82
No. of sales processed per person per day	8.5	2	4	12	8.5	9	10	12
Value of sales processes per person per day	£480	2	4	£750	£500	£600	680	£770
Total overtime worked per week (hr)	55	2	4	15	56	50	35	20
Staff morale rating (%)	68	3	6	80	70	72	74	75
Time spent with customers (hr/wk)	450	3	6	1,000	440	450	520	660
No. of new customers per period	3	4	7	10	3	4	3	7
No. of lost customers per period	5	4	7	2	5	4	4	3
Lead conversion rate (%)	28	4	8	40	25	33	33	33
Sales revenue	£300,000	4	9	£1m	£286,000	£275,000	£290,000	£350,000

Period = 3 months

Sales processing manager	
Customer relationship manager	
HR manager	
Sales manager	

Figure 13.3 Measure reporting – planned and actual – by stakeholder

the right-hand side of the map are not expected to improve for many months. Note that the measure for errors is a ratio and not an absolute value, since errors might increase if sales increased.

The reporting illustrated in Figure 13.3 highlights the interests of different stakeholders. An alternative, which highlights progress over time, is the benefits map.

The shading in Figure 13.4 represents a RAG status, with the addition of a fourth tint (which would usually be blue) to indicate that the benefit is not due to have reached its target. The map, appropriately coloured, would be presented every reporting period as a kind of dashboard. Figure 13.4 shows the status of the map one year after implementation of the new customer database and sales system.

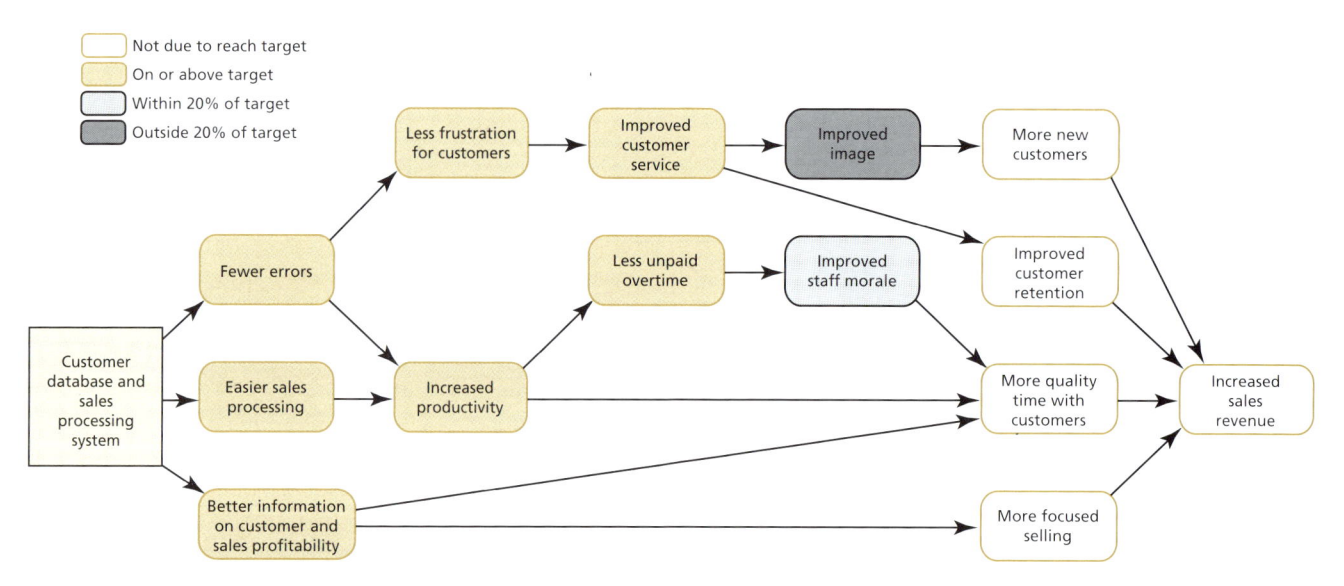

Figure 13.4 BRAG report (benefits map one year after implementation)

14 Documentation

14.1 THE PURPOSE OF DOCUMENTS

There are typically six main purposes for documents:

- To support recommendations and inform decisions
- To engage stakeholders and facilitate dialogue
- To communicate – intentions, plans and progress
- To educate, motivate and persuade
- To provide guidance (e.g. on process) and steer actions
- To record gathered information for future reference.

Templates are useful for recording and communicating information which fits a reasonably standard format. This standardization can facilitate data capture and certainly helps to ensure consistency in communication. Most of the documents required for managing portfolios, programmes and projects, incorporate templates. These templates are usually structured to:

- Highlight important characteristics
- Simplify understanding of relationships
- Facilitate comparisons and analysis.

The templates would normally occupy no more than a single sheet of paper. Examples of templates in the BRM space are:

- Strategy maps
- Benefits maps
- BDMs
- Benefit profiles
- Programme or project organizational structure
- Investment assessment matrices
- Trajectories
- Cost-benefit analysis calculations.

The documents in which these templates reside often contain several views of the data (sometimes involving different templates) together with analysis and, usually, conclusions and recommendations.

14.2 RANGE OF DOCUMENTS AND RELATIONSHIP BETWEEN THEM

Within change management literature (including PRINCE2 and MSP), more than 25 differently named documents are recommended to support the governance and management processes. It's unsurprising then that so many project and programme managers feel overwhelmed by the large number of reports they are required to produce (even though not all of these would be required for every programme).

Sometimes the aims of these documents are unclear, and they may overlap. Therefore, a set of overlapping documents could be consolidated into one, which would then evolve over time. The separate names, previously given to the unconsolidated documents, would then relate to snapshots of the new document, each of which would have a particular purpose and emphasis, depending on the stage in the lifecycle at which it is taken. Although, in theory, one 'big book' could replace all the documents, this would probably be a step too far and it could be impractical, bearing in mind the large number of contributors.

However, if the 'big book' was an integrated electronic database it could be extremely practical. The separate documents referred to in various change methodologies become nothing more than sophisticated reports from the database. This approach is not only very efficient but increases the consistency and integrity of the documents, making programme management and governance more effective and reliable.

Whether or not the documents are individually handcrafted or just generated from the integrated database, it may be helpful to consider their prime functions and any logical groupings. As a compromise between the idea of a single 'big book' and the 25+ named documents in the change management literature, at least one document should be expected for each of the five main programme themes:

- Benefit realization
- Stakeholder management
- Solution management
- Programme management
- Governance.

Figure 14.1 shows the documents used to support each of these themes, including in which of the six lifecycle phases they would first appear.

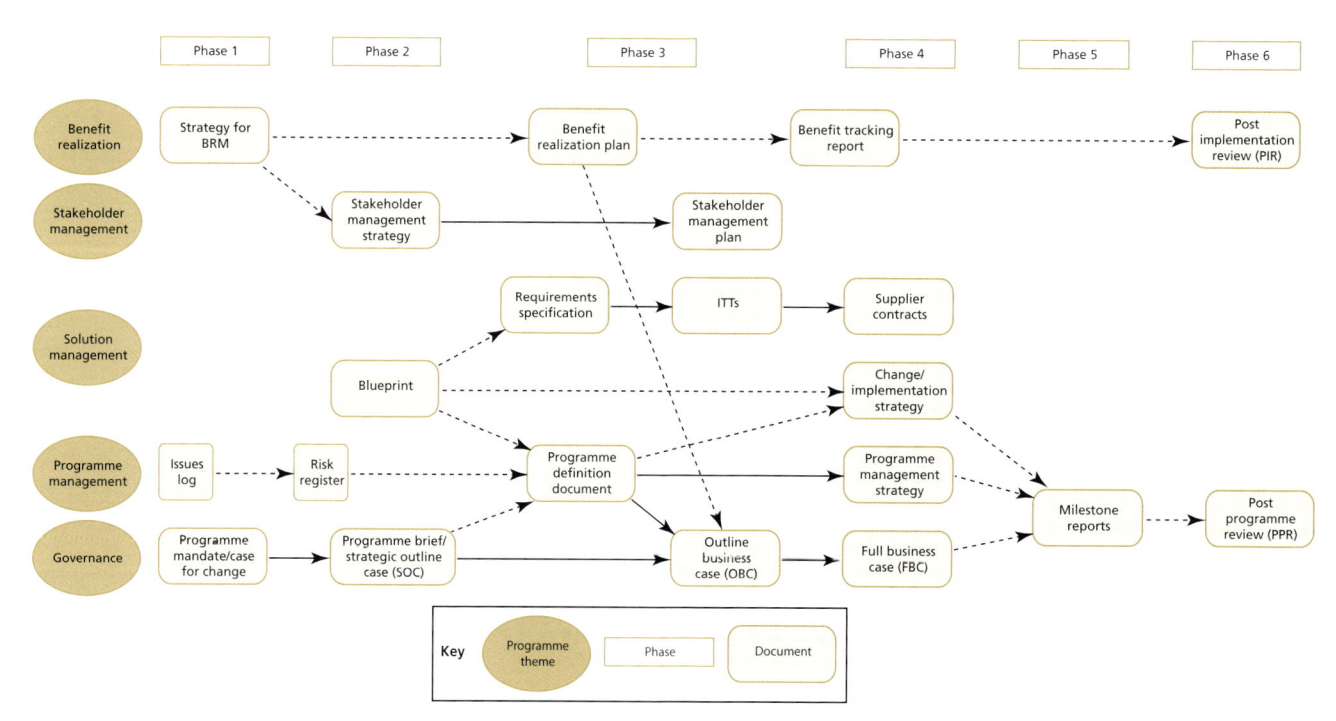

Figure 14.1 Common documents grouped by theme and phase

Documentation | 99

In Figure 14.1 the evolution of certain key documents is indicated by continual lines, while dotted lines indicate a contribution. A tabular version of this information is given in Figure 14.2.

The lifecycle diagram in Figure 14.3 shows which documents are likely to be considered at which review.

Phase when created or started	Document	Theme 1 Benefit realization	2 Stakeholder management	3 Solution management	4 Programme management	5 Governance
1	Strategy for change – sometimes known as programme mandate					■
1	Strategy for BRM – sometimes known as benefits management strategy	■	■			■
1	Issues log				■	
1	Risk register/log				■	
	Review					
2	Stakeholder management strategy		■			
2	Blueprint – sometimes known as business/target operating model			■		
2	Programme brief/strategic outline case (SOC)				■	■
	Review					
3	Benefit realization plan	■				
3	Stakeholder management plan (incl. communications strategy)		■			
3	Requirements definition document			■		
3	ITT/RFP			■		
3	Programme definition document:					
3	Governance/programme structure				■	■
3	Project initiation document(s)				■	
3	Programme plan				■	
3	Outline business case				■	■
	Review					
4	Benefit tracking report	■			■	■
4	Supplier contracts			■		
4	Change/implementation plan			■		
4	Programme management strategy			■		
4	Full business case					■
	Review					
5	Milestone reports				■	■
	Review					
6	Post-implementation review (PIR) report				■	■
6	Post-programme review (PPR) report	■			■	■
	Review					

Figure 14.2 Common documents grouped by theme and phase (tabular version)

Part 3: Elaboration of key techniques and responsibilities

- Post-implementation review
- Post-programme review

- Programme mandate
- Strategy for BRM
- Issues log and risk register

1. Set vision and objectives

2. Identify benefits and changes

- Stakeholder management strategy
- Blueprint
- Programme brief/strategic outline case

3. Define initiatives

- Benefit realization plan
- Stakeholder management plan
- Programme definition document
- Outline business case
- ITTs

4. Optimize initiatives

- Benefit tracking report
- Supplier contracts
- Programme management strategy
- Change implementation strategy
- Full business case

5. Manage initiatives

- Benefit tracking report
- Milestone reports

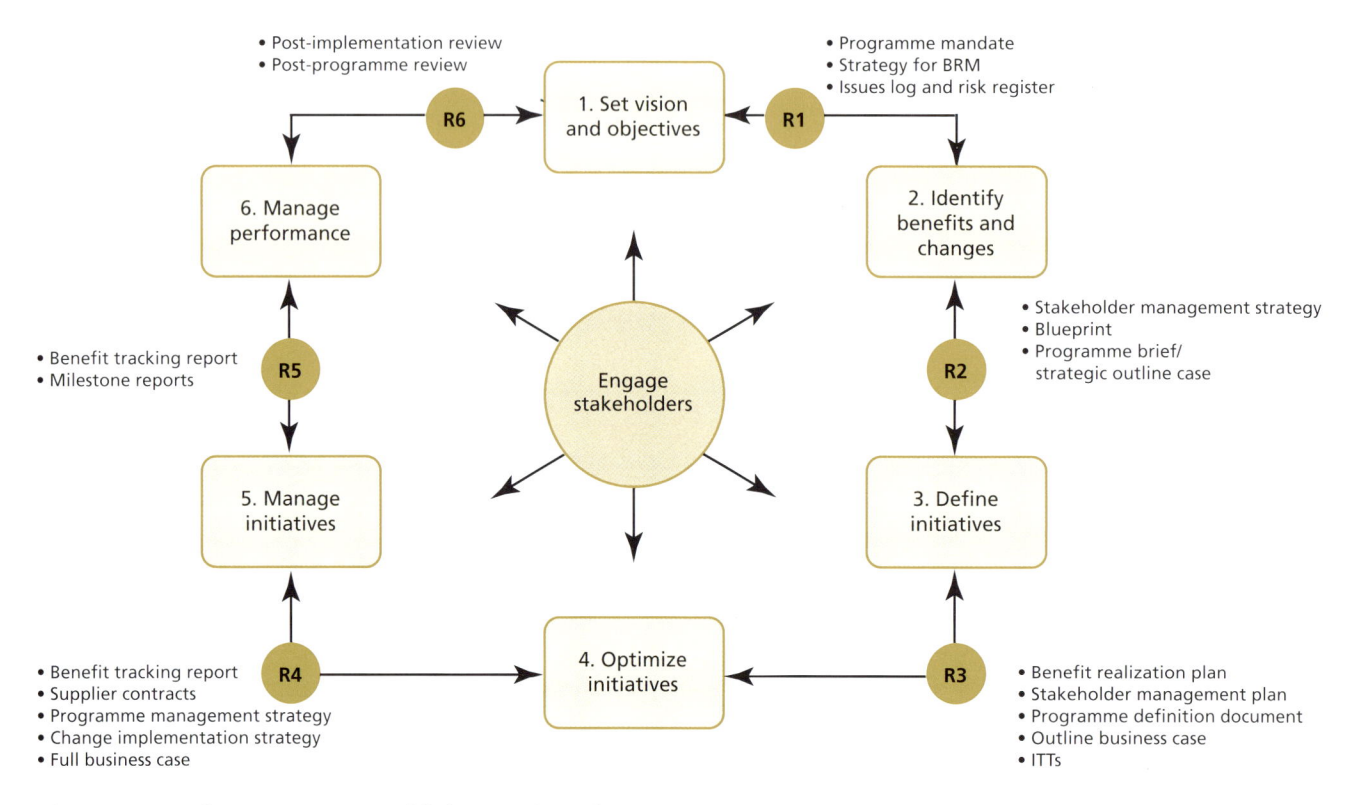

6. Manage performance

Engage stakeholders

Figure 14.3 Change process with key review documents

Part 4
Strategic organization-wide considerations

15 Portfolio management

15.1 THE SCOPE AND PURPOSE OF PORTFOLIO MANAGEMENT

Most organizations already have significant portfolios of investment in change, often comprising hundreds of projects and several programmes. There may be no shortage of activity or even investment, but does the organization have an optimum portfolio, taking account of its mission, goals, values, human resources, funds, and attitude to risk? Is the organization doing too much and achieving too little? The question is never more pertinent than in periods of economic instability and financial constraint.

It is vital that the change portfolio, like any investment portfolio, is actively managed in order to optimize the flow of benefits for the whole portfolio, relative to the degree of risk the organization is prepared to accept. As such, active portfolio management becomes a key part of embedding BRM within an organization which, in turn, is a key part of portfolio management.

Although most aspects of managing a portfolio of changes are very similar to those for managing a portfolio of shares there is one significant difference. Within a business environment there is an additional responsibility – that of creating and maintaining an overall environment in which the portfolio will thrive.

The primary objectives of portfolio management are:

1. To maximize the benefits realized from investment in change
2. To help deliver the organization's vision and goals as cost-effectively as possible.

These need to be underpinned by the following supporting objectives:

3. To define and communicate the environment for change – business strategy, values, guidelines, constraints, appetite for risk etc.
4. To create and maintain a high-value portfolio acceptable to the organization
5. To ensure appropriate guidance and support to those managing change – SROs, programme managers, project managers, benefit facilitators and business change managers
6. To ensure that the overall resources are distributed to generate the greatest return
7. To ensure stakeholders are engaged, involved and committed, but not overwhelmed by change.

Achieving objectives 3, 5, 6 and 7 should create an environment in which the portfolio will flourish, and achieving objective 4 should optimize the composition of the portfolio so that, together, objectives 3–7 should enable the fulfilment of the two primary objectives (1 and 2). These two aspects – of organizational environment and portfolio composition – are considered in detail in the following two sections.

15.2 CREATING AN ENVIRONMENT IN WHICH A CHANGE PORTFOLIO WILL FLOURISH

Creating the optimum environment, referred to as an 'energized change culture' in OGC's Portfolio Management Guide (PfM), has three main elements:

- Defining and clearly communicating the business strategy and goals, so that there is a clear context against which candidate programmes and projects can be assessed and compared – this may include KPIs and balanced scorecard indicators
- Engendering an innovative and questioning culture so that good new opportunities are identified and promoted
- Ensuring that suitable guidelines and support are available to increase the probability of success for each entrant (programme or project) to the portfolio.

Other influences or constraints which might need considering include:

- The organization's values
- The organization's attitude to, or appetite for, risk
- The business impact balance (based on the Cranfield Grid in Figure 4.5) considered appropriate for the organization
- Portfolio monitoring criteria for programmes and projects
- Pain thresholds – acceptable levels of change for stakeholders
- Resource constraints.

In order for the programme and project teams to operate effectively they will need to understand governance arrangements and the processes that need to be followed. In particular this will include an organization's:

- Change lifecycle (perhaps the one described in Chapter 3)
- Methodology for BRM – ideally a standard approach for the whole organization based on the ideas contained in this publication
- Methodology for programme and project management, perhaps based on guidance in MSP and PRINCE2
- Defined roles and responsibilities (see Chapter 11).

Although this whole framework will need to be reviewed and updated from time to time its initial definition is a one-off activity. Unlike the portfolio itself, it should not be continuously changing.

15.3 ACTIVE MANAGEMENT OF THE PORTFOLIO OF CHANGE

PfM highlights the continuous or cyclical nature of portfolio management and distinguishes between 'portfolio definition' and 'portfolio delivery'. The larger part of portfolio delivery comprises the individual delivery of the component programmes and projects and, as such, has been covered in the earlier chapters (particularly Chapters 4–9). The remaining aspects of delivery – monitoring the portfolio and taking remedial action – fit closely with portfolio definition and so are considered together as part of the active management of the portfolio, which involves:

- Regular monitoring of the current portfolio
- Investigating non-performing or poorly performing investments
- Correcting poorly managed programmes
- Closing programmes which are no longer in line with the organization's strategy
- Sanctioning only those new investments which will increase the overall value of the portfolio and maintain an appropriate risk balance.

As each of the above activities is undertaken in pursuit of the creation and maintenance of an optimum portfolio, the following nine factors must be reviewed and balanced:

- Degree of alignment with the organization's mission, strategy and policies
- Potential reward (desired benefits) – financial and non-financial
- Benefit timescales
- How well BRM is being applied
- Risk – especially of not achieving the benefits
- Business impact
- Organizational impact – especially the degree of change involved
- Resource requirements – especially business expertise
- Dependencies between investments.

Within a portfolio, the investments will be at different stages of their lifecycles, and so assessment of the above criteria, especially how well BRM is being applied, must take this into account. The assessments should be undertaken, if only briefly, for each regular review, and especially when new investments are being added to the portfolio. Additional in-depth annual reviews may be undertaken, perhaps by an independent review body.

When using these nine factors to assess a programme, particularly a potential new programme, there are two considerations:

- Does it stand up on its own as a worthwhile investment which supports the business strategy and direction?
- How does it score relative to other candidate (or possibly existing) programmes?

For the comparative assessment it may be helpful to create a score for each of the nine factors listed above and then compute a weighted total.

15.4 RESPONSIBILITY FOR PORTFOLIO MANAGEMENT

Responsibility for portfolio management is spread across many different roles including those responsible for the individual components of the portfolio – programme, project and change managers. However, in this section, the focus is on the key roles of the portfolio board and the portfolio management office (PMO), elaborating on the guidance contained in section 11.2.

15.4.1 Portfolio board

In many organizations the complete portfolio of change activities will affect the majority of staff from within the organization and impact many stakeholders from outside the organization. As a result, effective management of this portfolio will require top-level leadership, perhaps coming from the main board, in view of:

- The number and diversity of stakeholders who must be influenced
- The magnitude and source of the required funding
- The enormity of the potential rewards
- The related risks and change impacts.

Although this leadership should start with the main board, active monitoring and management of the portfolio may be delegated to a subset of the board or to a group one level below board level. The toughness of some of the decisions to be taken (for example, killing a pet project) demands seniority.

A portfolio containing several hundred investments is almost unmanageable, especially by a single portfolio board. In this situation projects should be synergistically grouped into a much smaller number of programmes and/or a hierarchy of portfolio boards should be used.

The main responsibilities of the portfolio board are to:

- Define and communicate parameters of the change environment (a one-off)
- Encourage a culture of new ideas – creativity, continual improvement
- Identify and sponsor initiatives needed to deliver the organization's vision
- Review and then reject or sanction new proposals
- Monitor continuously the whole portfolio
- Terminate programmes and projects that are not performing or are no longer fit for purpose.

To be effective, the portfolio board should meet frequently (usually monthly). It will need practical support from a group of analysts, administrators and facilitators (normally referred to as the portfolio management office or PMO) plus the commitment of many other professionals, such as programme, project and business change managers, together with the support of a much wider group of stakeholders.

15.4.2 Portfolio management office

The PMO is defined in P3O® (The Stationery Office, 2008) as a: 'Permanent office set up to support the definition and delivery of a portfolio of change across the entire organization or enterprise.'

The primary roles of the PMO are to:

- Support the portfolio board in its decision making
- Support the portfolio board in its wider influence, especially with stakeholders.

Possible secondary roles include:

- Becoming a centre of expertise for BRM and PPM
- Becoming a resource pool for programme and project managers.

Even when these secondary roles are not part of the PMO, it must still maintain close relationships with the groups responsible for these activities.

In its primary roles of supporting the portfolio board, the PMO will need to:

- Evaluate new programme and project proposals using agreed criteria:
  - Checking alignment and contribution to corporate strategy and goals
  - ROI
  - Proposed application of BRM (e.g. strategy for BRM)
  - Risks
- Check mix/balance with existing portfolio:
  - Cranfield Grid
  - Resource requirements
  - Stakeholder impact
- Oversee and consolidate performance reporting of existing portfolio
- Investigate those programmes or projects which are missing targets for change or benefits
- Identify candidates for removal from the portfolio
- Prepare reports and recommendations for the portfolio board.

Several of these responsibilities require input from the benefit facilitator role so it makes sense for the benefit facilitator role to sit within the PMO. Figure 15.1 summarizes the structure.

Portfolio management | **107**

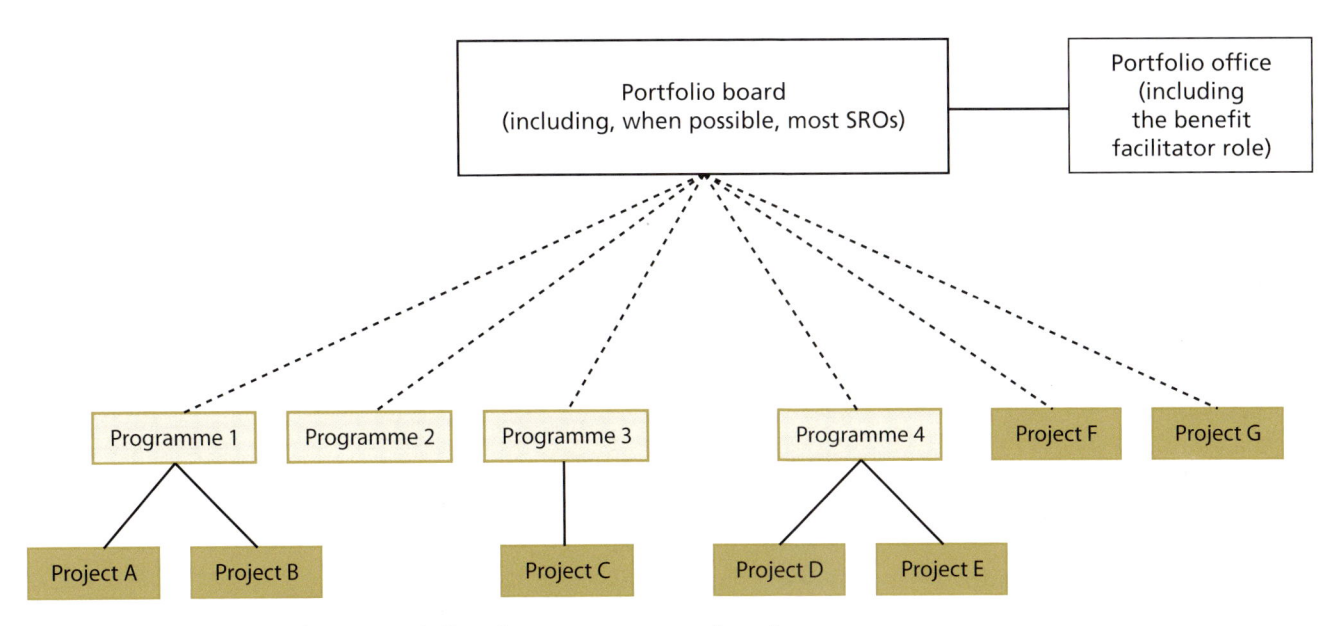

Figure 15.1 Structure for a portfolio of programmes and projects

15.5 GETTING STARTED

If your organization already has a portfolio board and a PMO then you may wish to use this chapter to check for any gaps in responsibilities or activities. If these are not in place, then establishing them is a significant task, which may involve considerable changes to the way the organization functions. This transition should be managed as a programme, with an SRO, programme board, programme manager and appropriate funding. An alternative would be to manage these changes as a distinct project within the wider programme of embedding BRM in the organization (see Chapter 16).

In either situation it would be appropriate to apply BRM to this change activity, engaging stakeholders, identifying and mapping the benefits and required changes, managing the implementation of the changes and tracking and reporting the benefits.

A fuller treatment of portfolio management is provided in PfM.

16 Embedding BRM within an organization

16.1 THE NEED TO EMBED BRM

It is very important to embed BRM within the organization for the following reasons:

- If BRM is applied to just one or two projects or programmes there is a real risk that it may fade away once these projects have completed. There are private-sector organizations that enthusiastically applied BRM techniques to a few projects in the early 1990s, yet 15 years later were doing very little with it. Embedding BRM will change the cultural mindset and provide ongoing reinforcement and commitment.
- If BRM is applied patchily or inconsistently across the organization it makes effective portfolio management extremely difficult, if not impossible. Portfolio management needs consistent approaches to both the management and tracking of benefits in order to make meaningful comparisons and to have confidence that predicted benefits will actually be realized.
- The ROI of BRM is so enormous (see Section 1.7) that it would be irresponsible not to see it applied as widely as possible in an organization. It is unlikely that the organization has any other investments giving anything like the same returns.

16.2 THE PROCESS OF EMBEDDING

The process of embedding should not be regarded lightly. Although BRM is largely common sense it is not common practice and requires a widespread change of mindset which implies significant cultural change. This will be difficult to achieve without top-level sponsorship, commitment, patience and appropriate funding.

In view of the nature, timescale and breadth of the impact of this change, it is best to manage the embedding process as a programme with an SRO, programme board, programme manager, business change manager and budget.

Although top-level commitment is required for the complete embedding of BRM across an organization, it is not always easy to secure this commitment at the outset. Winning senior hearts and minds may have to be a gradual process (see the case study in Chapter 17).

One way to influence senior managers is to generate, as early as possible, some significant internal success stories, so as part of the proposed change programme it is recommended that the BRM approach is piloted on two or three programmes or projects, preferably ones with distinctly different characteristics.

To ensure these pilots are successful it may be worth securing external help from consultants with a track record in BRM to at least help with the first three phases.

A functional view of some of the activities comprising a programme to embed BRM is illustrated in Figure 16.1. The sequence in which these activities are undertaken will depend on the characteristics and needs of the particular organization. However, it is likely that several of these activities can be managed in parallel.

Embedding BRM within an organization | 109

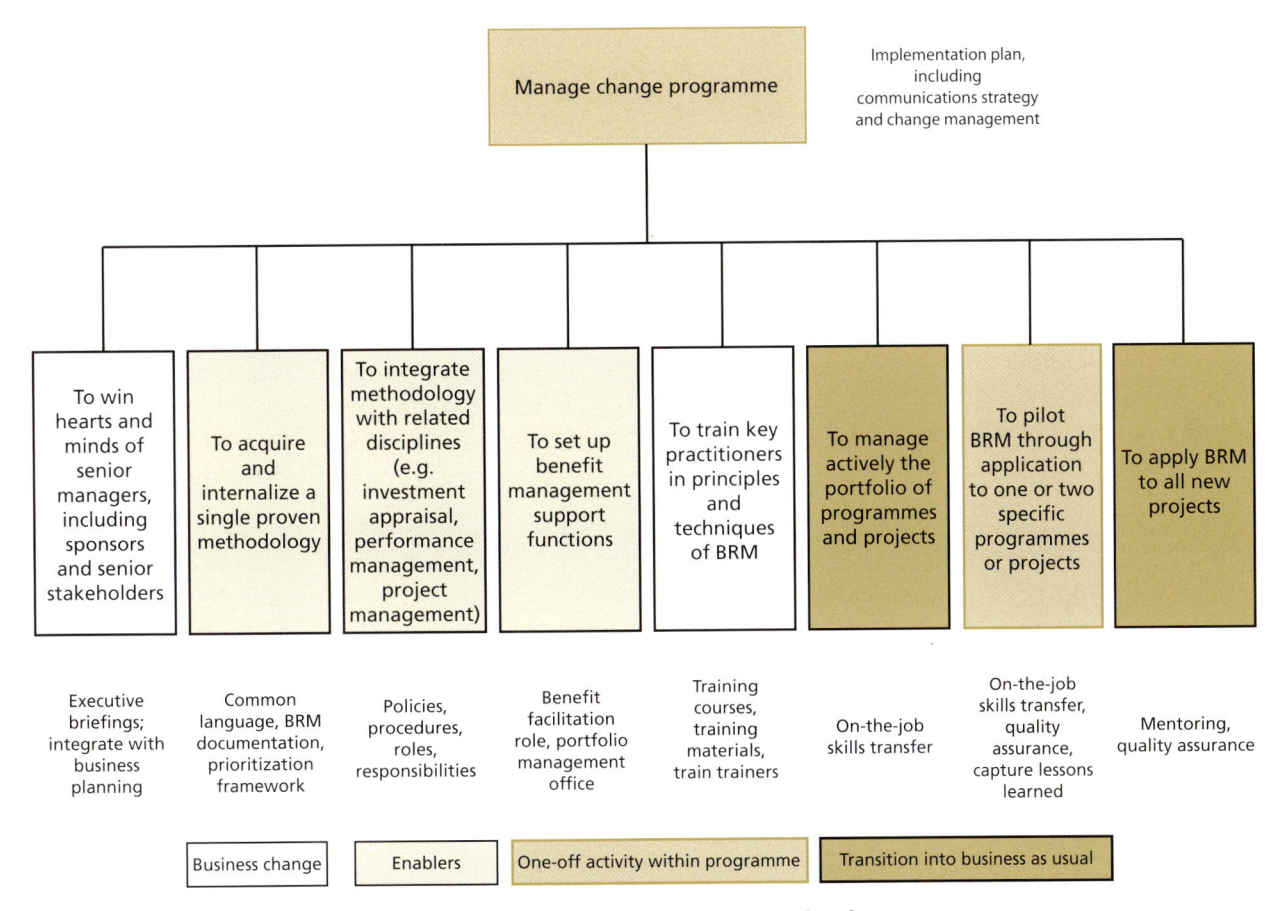

Figure 16.1 Activity themes for embedding BRM within an organization

16.3 APPLYING BRM TO THE EMBEDDING PROCESS

If, as suggested, the embedding of BRM is being managed as a programme, then BRM should be applied to the programme as it would be to any other programme, and the lifecycle recommended in Chapter 3 adopted.

The embedding of BRM should involve workshops and the production of a set of maps. Figures 4.2 and 16.2 are examples of maps that may be used in this process.

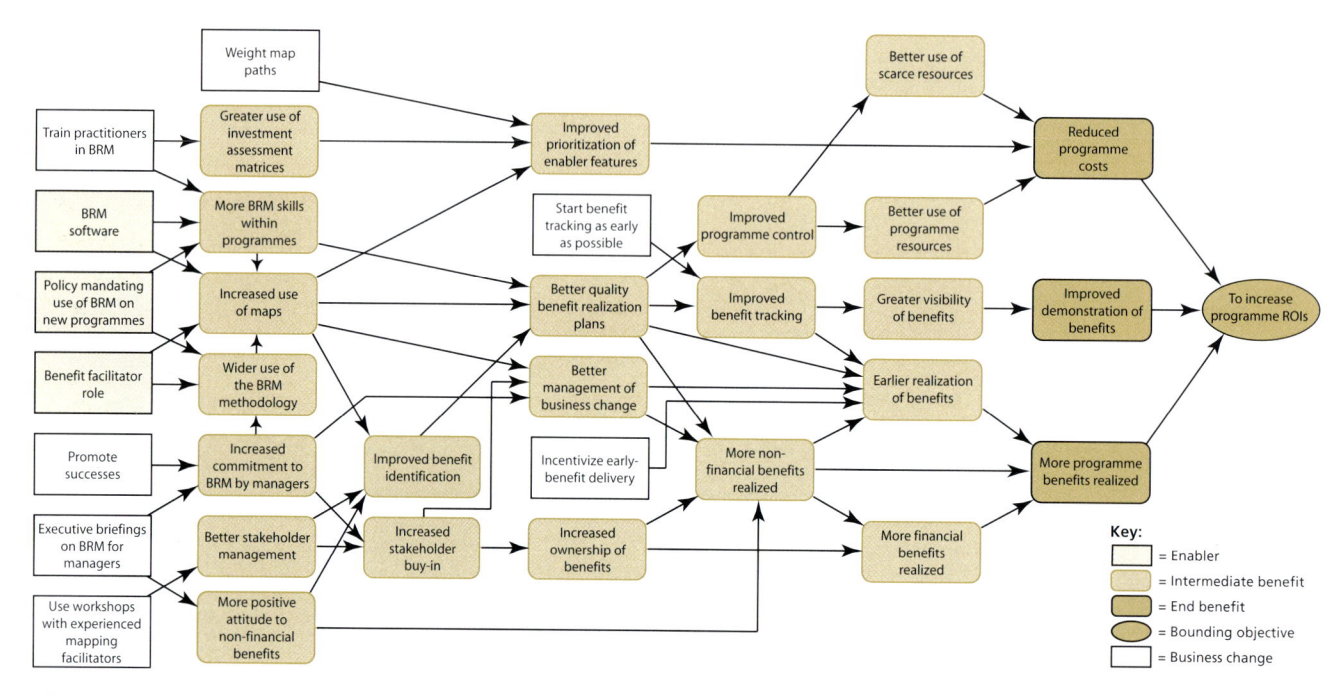

Part 4: Strategic organization-wide considerations

Figure 16.2 BDM for objective 'to increase programme ROIs'

17 Case study: the British Council

17.1 INTRODUCTION

The British Council's programme support office ran its first benefits workshop in September 2007, five months after attending a benefits realization management seminar. During the following two years it worked with Sigma to enhance its understanding of benefits realization. It has come a long way, but still has some way to go. This is the story of the British Council's journey so far.

17.2 THE BACKGROUND

The British Council has worked for 75 years to build engagement and trust for the UK internationally. We work in 110 countries, connecting with millions of people through programmes in the arts, education, science, sport and the English language.

Our small unit has existed since 2003, set up as a centre of excellence for programme management to support the biggest change programme that the British Council had ever undertaken – a programme to restructure our entire operation overseas and in the UK, and to move to a different model of regional and global delivery supported by the roll-out of an integrated finance and business system.

We set out to deliver this change professionally using MSP methodology. We built a risks database, trained people, developed plans and a reporting process – we seemed well on track to deliver the benefits described in our various business cases.

And we undoubtedly did deliver many of those benefits – but some we didn't deliver and some we could have delivered if we'd identified them all in the first place. It was the most important part of what we were doing, but the part that, like so many organizations, we could have done better. As time went on, senior managers wanted to see evidence of benefits being delivered from this major initiative, but we were struggling to provide a full picture.

17.3 BACK TO THE DRAWING BOARD

In April 2007 our unit head attended a Sigma BRM workshop with two of our senior programme managers – all three came back full of enthusiasm for what they'd heard and were inspired to reassess our approach to benefits.

Ideally, of course, new initiatives start with a mandate from senior managers but, in reality, it's not always like that. Our senior managers were receptive to talking about a new approach to benefits. They were impressed by the BRM approach, but not yet ready to take on another major new initiative at that point.

So we decided that the unit would take a different approach. We'd work with our own constituency of programme managers to introduce BRM into the organization through them. We'd take it slowly; see what worked and what didn't. Gerald Bradley calls it 'sowing seeds to change the culture'. Our unit head described it as 'lighting fires'. Our longer term hope was that the British Council's next major strategic initiative would start with some benefits mapping.

17.4 LIGHTING FIRES

From April 2007 we started to light the fires. We commissioned various external consultants to work with the change programmes that had already started to try and 'retro-fit' benefits. This worked better for some than for others. Much of it was frustrating and, at times, felt like wasted work. At the very least though, programme managers exposed to the approach were generally positive about using it in the future. Significantly:

- Our network of overseas programme managers was particularly enthusiastic – and overseas is where we deliver most of our work
- We started work on benefits with two major programmes that were just beginning.

17.4.1 Help with lighting fires

In October 2007 we contracted an external consultant to help us move further forward with embedding BRM in the organization. That was the beginning of a systematic 'fire lighting' programme which included:

- Mapping the benefits we expected to get from our own project to embed BRM into the organization (practice what you preach)
- Nurturing our programme managers' network to bring them along with us
- Running benefits workshops in the UK with new programmes
- Building our reach overseas, including workshops in Vienna and Ukraine
- Starting work on our BRM processes and delivery toolkit
- Building and training a small group of internal benefits workshop facilitators
- Attending benefits forums and advanced workshops to learn more from the experts and from the BRM community of practitioners
- Updating ourselves on the place of BRM in the new version of MSP.

17.5 MAPPING AT A STRATEGIC LEVEL

By April 2008 we'd covered a lot of ground. Then we were asked to help support the team developing the British Council's next organizational strategy. Our hope that benefits mapping would be included in this process was fulfilled.

We did face an immediate challenge. It was impossible to get our key stakeholders (four busy members of our executive board plus various senior people based overseas) together in one room to develop a benefits dependency map. If we wanted to stay involved with the process we'd have to be creative. We did this by constructing maps from records of interviews, conversations and meetings then checking back with everyone to see if it looked right – lengthy but effective.

It would be wrong of us to claim that the development of this organizational strategy was primarily driven by a classic BRM approach – it wasn't. But some important elements of BRM were involved – a big step forward.

17.6 TAKING THE BENEFITS INITIATIVE

Our external consultant stayed with us for longer than we had anticipated, mainly because of their involvement over a number of months in strategic mapping. As the time came for us to take over completely we made sure that we had finished all the tasks in our plan, including:

- Making sure that our benefits facilitators had their final training sessions
- Getting our BRM toolkit finished
- Running a major benefits workshop for our East Asia region.

By early December we were on our own – but feeling more confident than we'd anticipated about taking the benefits agenda forward alone.

17.7 WHAT DID WE LEARN?

We learned a huge amount of technical things about BRM, which were invaluable in making us more skilled and professional. Equally importantly though we learned:

- That it's not essential to have a specific senior management mandate for introducing BRM. It was enough to be allowed to have a go, to influence people to try BRM and to let it speak for itself. In fact, doing it that way was arguably more, rather than less, powerful.
- How to tackle 'the lurch' – the point after the 'intellectual conversion' when the hard work of thrashing out the practicalities begins and measures and ownership have to be agreed. A major benefit of BRM is it makes accountability very clear, but that's also a potential disbenefit – it's very exposing and potentially uncomfortable. We had to try and take people through that, and we have to admit that we didn't succeed every time.
- The importance of having an embedded consultant for this work. This helped us at every stage to see how BRM theory could, without losing its underlying rigour, be adapted to work in a variety of real-life situations.
- To be adaptable. We thought that we would be trained to run a series of standard BRM workshops. Instead we learned to adapt what we were doing at each stage so that we could take people with us.
- How to use our programme managers as BRM champions.
- To be patient – some people started the process, dropped it and then later came back to it.
- To deal with all the benefits workshop equipment, including transport by cab and plane!

17.8 THE FUTURE

We've now got a practical framework in place. We've won various hearts and minds and influenced people. We hear conversations couched in benefits language and see people using benefits maps as a standard part of what they are doing.

We did learn that, for our organization, big stakeholder workshops are not always the best way forward. Other organizations say the opposite. It's a question of taking the basic principles of BRM and adapting it to your own situation.

We would be the first to admit that the journey isn't over, although we've come a long way. We may even have to lay low for a while before our next 'push' to get BRM more firmly embedded within our organization. We'll carry on being realistic and pragmatic and using our influencing skills – we've found that it's by far the best way to make progress.

Further information

Glossary

Further information

Bradley, Gerald (2010) *Benefit Realisation Management: A practical guide to achieving benefits though change,* Gower Publishing, ISBN 9781409400943

Jenner, Stephen (2009) *Realising Benefits from Government ICT Investment – a fool's errand?* Academic Publishing International, ISBN 9781906638269

Office of Government Commerce (2007) *Managing Successful Programmes,* TSO, ISBN 9780113310401

Office of Government Commerce (2008) 'Portfolio Management Guide'. Available online at www.ogc.gov.uk/delivery_lifecycle_portfolio_management.asp. To be replaced by a publication coming from TSO in early 2011.

Office of Government Commerce (2008), *Portfolio, Programme and Project Offices,* TSO, ISBN 9780113311248

Office of Government Commerce (2009), *Managing Successful Projects with PRINCE2™,* TSO, ISBN 9780113310593

Glossary

Some of the following glossary terms are accompanied by italicized text, in which the author elaborates upon how that term is used within the context of benefits realization.

added value
Value which is additional to cost reduction.

attribute of a benefit
A characteristic of a benefit (e.g. business impact, category, value type, value, expected time of realization, beneficiary, accountable stakeholder, risk).

These are gathered together in a benefit profile.

balanced business scorecard
A balanced business scorecard is a scorecard for monitoring business performance.

This is normally divided into four quadrants: customer, development/learning, internal improvement and finance.

baseline
Reference levels against which an entity is monitored and controlled.

The point in time is normally during the planning/ justification phase of a proposed investment in change.

benchmark
An industry standard for a particular measure, often used to determine a target.

beneficiaries
People who will feel or experience the value of a benefit.

benefit dependency map
A benefit dependency map (BDM) is a benefits map with the addition of dependencies – enablers and business changes.

A map which links primary objectives to the enabling technology and business change, and so charts the activities on which the benefits depend.

benefit distribution matrix
An illustration of the distribution of benefits against disbenefits across the organization, i.e. the winners and losers in a change.

This is a frequently used example of an investment assessment matrix.

benefit facilitator
A centre of expertise for BRM to support programmes and projects with benefit realization yet challenge benefit claims and business cases.

The role should be a permanent role within an organization, sitting outside individual programmes and best located in the portfolio office.

benefit management
The identification, definition, tracking, realization and optimization of benefits, usually within a programme.

The name previously used for BRM and still used by some organizations.

benefit owner

A person responsible for the realization of a benefit.

benefit profile

The template which contains the comprehensive description of a single benefit, including all its attributes and dependencies.

It includes all the information – precise definition, attributes, system and business dependencies, and measurement criteria – needed to aid realization. Ideally this information should be contained in a single page.

benefit realization management

Benefit realization management (BRM) is the process of organizing and managing, so that potential benefits, arising from investment in change, are actually achieved.

It is a continuous process running through the whole change lifecycle and should be the central theme of any change initiative, whether applied to the whole portfolio, a programme or a project.

benefit realization management process

The process for applying BRM. This is effectively the process for managing change.

This is subdivided into six phases with a recommended review point at the close of each phase.

benefit realization plan

A benefit realization plan (BRP) is a complete view of all the benefit profiles in the form of a schedule.

The document would be the handbook of the sponsor and of value to stakeholders, the programme team and those accountable for the realization of specific benefits.

benefit trajectory

A time sequence of benefits.

A stream of expected benefits values.

benefits bucket

A corporate or portfolio 'pot' for a particular type or category of benefit.

This pot would be established corporately in the expectation that a number of programmes or projects will contribute to it. It is not dissimilar to a key performance indicator.

benefits map

A network of benefits, usually linked to one or more of the bounding investment objectives, which maps all the cause-and-effect relationships.

Its status will evolve through: wishlist, set of feasible paths, plan of selected options, visual for communicating intentions and benefit tracking mechanism.

blueprint

A model of the future business or organization, its working practices and processes, the information it requires and the technology that will be needed to deliver the capability described in the vision statement.

A benefit dependency map is an early and high-level view of a blueprint.

bounding objectives
The set of end objectives (usually three or four) defining the boundary of a programme or project

BRAG status
Like a RAG status but including blue for 'not yet due to reach target'.

business case
The justification for an organizational activity (strategic, programme, project, operational) which typically contains costs, benefits, risks and timescales and against which continuing viability is tested.

It should describe and value the expected benefits, specify the costs covering enablers and business changes and include a map of how the change is expected to realize the benefits.

business change
A change which occurs within the business/operational environment; often a new way of working or a new business state, which may utilize a new enabler.

A task, process or piece of work intended to produce a new business state or a benefit. It should be defined so that it could have definite start and end dates and someone responsible.

capability
A service, function or operation that enables the organization to exploit opportunities.

For example – new staff (enablers) are trained and developed (business change) to become a skilled team (capability).

change
The set of actions by which the organization moves from any current state to any desired state.

Changes may also be grouped into work packages, projects, tranches and programmes.

change initiative
A change delivery mechanism, such as a portfolio, programme or project.

change lifecycle
The lifecycle of a change initiative.

consequential benefit
A benefit arising as a consequence of having achieved a programme objective.

A benefit to which the programme contributes but which may be shared with other projects or programmes.

customers
Individuals and organizations that buy and/or receive products and services.

disbenefit
Outcomes perceived as negative by one or more stakeholders. Disbenefits are actual consequences of an activity whereas, by definition, a risk has some uncertainty about whether it will materialize.

driver
Some internal or external pressure or opportunity which is stimulating or driving the need for change.

enabler

An enabler is something that can be developed/built/acquired normally from outside the environment in which it will be embedded and where the benefits will be realized.

An enabler is normally costed, budgeted and formally planned, usually within a project or programme. Enablers include: IT systems, communications systems, buildings, policies, procedures and skills.

end benefit

One of a set of benefits which collectively are equivalent to a bounding objective.

end objective

The ultimate objective of a change initiative. Usually beyond the boundary of what the change is directly accountable for.

goal

A general term for the purpose of change, which may be any combination of vision, objectives and benefits.

governance structure

The organization and processes needed to govern a programme.

intermediate benefits

Benefits which will occur between the implementation of early changes and the realization of the end benefits.

investment assessment matrix

An investment assessment matrix (IAM) is a matrix of benefits used for checking balance and alignment, and for optimizing the worth of a programme.

The axes of the matrix are benefit attributes taken from the benefit profile.

key performance indicator

Metric (either financial or non-financial) that is used to set and measure progress towards strategic objectives for an organization.

lifecycle

The series of events in the life of a project or programme.

Managing Successful Programmes (MSP)

A TSO publication written by OGC giving guidance on programme management.

measure

A quantity, derived from a set of metrics, whose change in the desired direction would help to confirm that the related benefit is being realized.

The measure is the thing that will be tracked and monitored (e.g. 'value of monthly sales'). It is not the value (e.g. £300,000), the target (e.g. +30%), the means of measurement (e.g. quarterly financial review) or the benefit (e.g. more sales).

measure monitor

The role of gathering and consolidating the ongoing monitoring and reporting of the raw measurement data.

metric
A raw piece of data, often captured by a computer system, from which measures may be derived.

This could be the basic statistics of each call made to a call centre or details of every sale.

milestone
A significant event or stage in a project.

mission
The purpose for which the organization exists.

net present value
100 x (benefits DCF − costs DCF)/costs DCF, where DCF is discounted cash flow.

objective
A statement of purpose, which is specific and carries clear intent. An answer to the 'why' question.

A major component of the transition from current state to blueprint expressed as an aim or purpose.

optimization
A benefit-driven process which exploits all types of opportunity for increasing the value of an investment.

phase
One of the six subdivisions of the BRM/change process.

portfolio
All the programmes and standalone projects being undertaken by an organization, a group of organizations or an organizational unit.

The portfolio may relate to the whole organization or to a major subdivision. Ideally the mix of initiatives will be balanced in respect of size, complexity, risk and reward.

portfolio board
The senior-level board responsible for managing the whole change portfolio.

Sometimes referred to as: steering group, sponsoring group or change management executive.

portfolio office
The office responsible for supporting the portfolio board in the managing of the whole change portfolio.

The benefit facilitator role fits comfortably into this office.

Portfolio, Programme and Project Offices (P3O)
This is the OGC term for an office or a hierarchy of offices to support portfolio, programme or project management.

predicted value
An alternative term for 'target' preferred by many organizations.

programme
A temporary flexible organization structure created to coordinate, direct and oversee the implementation of a set of related projects and activities in order to deliver benefits related to the organization's strategic objectives. A programme is likely to have a life that spans several years.

The total investment or package of change designed to achieve the primary objectives in support of the vision.

programme board

A group that supports the senior responsible owner to deliver the programme.

This board should comprise senior representatives of the key stakeholders and be chaired by the SRO.

programme management

The coordinated organization, direction and implementation of a dossier of projects and activities that together achieve outcomes and realize benefits that are of strategic importance.

project

A temporary organization that is created for the purpose of delivering one or more business products according to an agreed business case.

RAG status

Red, amber and green status – colours used to indicate closeness to target.

Green: on or close to target; amber: a wider deviation from target; red: well off target

request for proposal

Request for a proposal – for products or services.

Sometimes referred to as an invitation to tender (ITT).

requirement definition process

A formal process for defining change requirements, usually for a computer system.

The creation of a BDM is a good example of initial 'requirements definition'.

resources

People, equipment, money.

return on investment

The return for a particular investment, usually expressed as a percentage of the outlay.

score

A ranking or relative weight attached to an entity, usually a benefit, from applying percentage weights to the paths of a map.

senior responsible owner

A senior responsible owner (SRO) is the UK government term for the individual responsible for ensuring that a project or programme of change meets its objectives and delivers the projected benefits. The person should be the owner of the overall business change that is being supported by the programme or project.

The senior responsible owner (SRO) should ensure that the change maintains its business focus, that it has clear authority, and that the context, including risks, is actively managed. The SRO should be recognized as the owner throughout the organization.

sponsor

The main driving force behind a programme or project.

This is likely to be the person who has put up, or at least sanctioned, the funding and is ultimately responsible and accountable for the effective fulfilment of a programme or project, including the realization of benefits. This role is undertaken by the SRO, as part of the sponsoring group, in the MSP environment.

stakeholder

Any individual, group or organization that can affect, be affected by, or perceive itself to be affected by, an initiative (programme, project, activity, risk).

Stakeholders should normally include customers, suppliers (internal or external) and anyone who can throw a spanner in the works.

strategy map

A high-level (strategic) map showing a set of objectives linked in 'cause-and-effect' relationships.

These maps will normally show the 'bounding objectives' and the 'boundary' of the change initiative (e.g. programme).

target

A defined end point, normally expressed as a numeric value.

This is generally applied to objectives, benefits and measures.

vision

A concise description/picture of the desired future state of an organization or organizational unit, resulting from planned change.

The planned change may be managed as a portfolio of programmes, a single programme, a project, a work package or a combination of these.

weighted paths

A map path which has been weighted (usually as a percentage) relative to other paths to signify its relative importance for further investment.

yield

The annual return from an investment.

Index

Index

acceptance testing 57
action, influencing 89
actual return on investment (AROI)
   maximizing 4, 8
   see also return on investment (ROI)
added value 7
   definition 118
alignment of programme and business objectives 24, 25, 50–4, 104
attribute of a benefit, definition 118

balance see portfolio balance
balanced business scorecard
   category 91
   definition 118
   indicators 103
baseline, definition 89, 118
benchmark
   data 45, 46
   definition 89, 118
beneficiaries, definition 118
benefit dependency map (BDM) 35, 43, 44, 84, 85
   British Council 112
   definition 118
benefit distribution matrix 33, 34, 67
   definition 118
benefit facilitator 17, 27, 39, 47, 48, 56
   British Council 112, 113
   definition 118
   role and responsibilities 57, 58, 73, 77, 94
benefit management
   definition 118–19
   vs benefit realization 4
benefit measures see measures
benefit owner 44, 76, 91
   definition 119
   role and responsibilities 57, 58, 61, 73
benefit profile 44, 45
   definition 119
benefit realization
   accountability for 73
   effective 10, 14, 18
   importance and value 3–4
   tracking 8
benefit realization management (BRM)
   adaptability 113
   as an investment 8
   case study 111–13
   centrality to effective change 12
   dangers of inconsistent application 108
   definition 119
   embedding within an organization 108–10
   essentials 15–17
   increasing importance 6–8
   iterative nature 11
   methodology 104
   purpose and scope 4–5
   return on investment (ROI) 9, 108
   scalability 4–5, 13
   in scoping change 5, 18
   standard approach 12–13
   strategy for applying 9, 27
   terminology 3–4
benefit realization management process, definition 119
benefit realization manager 17, 77
benefit realization plan (BRP) 37, 38–9, 47
   definition 119
   promoting and packaging 55
benefit trajectory, definition 119

benefit-measure contribution 90–1
benefits
    attributes 53
    beneficiaries 52, 67, 90
    categorization 70–1
    classifications 66–71
    definition 65
    delayed realization 7
    describing 29–30, 65
    early 55
    economic value 72
    financial value 68–70, 71
    identifying 7, 16, 29–33
    'key' 37, 92–4
    mapping 29–33, 111, 112, 113
    measurable 66
    measuring 28, 92–4
    non-financial 4, 14, 18, 52, 68–70, 72
    as outcome of change 66
    ranking 42
    realization 7, 75
    reporting 47
    Sigma value type 67–70
    stakeholder impact 67
    tracking and reporting 17, 44–7, 50, 55–6, 61, 75, 95–6
    validating 44–7, 71
    valuation 44–7, 71–2
benefits bucket 91
    definition 119
benefits map 28, 29, 30, 32, 33, 80, 83, 93, 95
    definition 119
benefits workshops *see* workshops
blueprint 6, 11, 35, 37, 38, 42–3
    definition 119
    development 75
bounding objectives 22–4, 28, 31, 35, 80
    definition 120
    scoring 84

BRAG status 56, 95–6
    definition 120
brainstorming 29, 30
British Council (case study) 111–13
business case 21, 44
    approval 17
    definition 120
    developing 48
business change
    definition 66, 120
    effective 6
    funding 57
    implementing 12, 57
    key roles 57
    management 44
    prioritizing and costing 17
    see also change(s)
business change manager 47, 48, 49
    role and responsibilities 57, 58, 73, 76
business environments, complexity 7
business impact
    assessing 67
    classification 53–4
business as usual, smooth transition 42, 57, 60

capability, definition 66, 120
'cart before the horse' mentality 10
cash flow 44
change(s)
    case for 26–7
    constraints 104
    costing 44
    definition 120
    determining 75
    drivers 5
    identifying 33–6
    impact on business performance 3
    investment in 3, 4
    managing 3

overcoming resistance to 58–9
programme 4
type 71
see also business change
change champion, role and responsibilities 57, 58, 76
change initiative 3
definition 120
change lifecycle
definition 120
iterative nature 18
phases 15
change management literature 97–8
change portfolio
active management 104–5
optimum environment 103–4
communication
importance 12, 65
see also language; visual communication
computing, historical perspective 7
consequential benefit 31
definition 120
cost
of applying BRM 8–9
of change 17, 40–4
of measurement 93–4
reduction 7, 9
cost benefit analysis, limited value 7
Cranfield Grid 26, 29, 30, 50, 52, 67, 72
customers, definition 120

database, use for reporting 98
decision making 89
disbenefits
definition 65, 120
identifying 12, 30, 57
minimizing impact 12, 33, 57
stakeholder impact 67
stakeholder perception 58–9

documentation 97–100
documents, logical groupings 98–100
drivers
for change 80
definition 120
duplicate entities, identifying and consolidating 17, 28, 36

enabler benefits 30
enabler project 77
enablers 5, 6
acquisition 17
building/acquisition 75
capacity to deliver objectives 79–80
definition 66, 121
delivery 57
duplicate 17
focus on 10
implementing 12
integration 11
linking to business change 87
end benefits 31, 33, 39, 82–3
definition 121
tracking 94
end goal *see* goal
end objective
definition 121
see also objectives
energized change culture 103
existing environment 21
external consultants 111–13
external suppliers 7, 43, 44

feeder benefits 45, 83, 91
focus, checking 50
functionality
additional to specification 54
optimizing 55
relation to benefits 44

funding, securing 48–9

gateways *see* reviews
global economy 7
goal
    definition 121
    establishing 5, 75
    generic term for purpose of change 66
    see also vision statement
governance structure, definition 121

historical perspective 7
'how' questions 21

improvements
    prioritizing 84–6
    timescale 90, 91
in-depth reviews 105
industry-recognized process 12
initiatives
    defining 17, 40–9
    managing 57
    optimizing 50–6
intermediate benefits 31, 33, 83
    definition 121
internal consistency, checking 50–4
investment
    in change 3, 4
    focusing 6
    scoping 5–6, 7
    wasted 8, 50, 80
investment assessment matrix (IAM) 51, 52, 53
    definition 121
invitation to tender (ITT) 43, 44
    definition 123
issues log 27, 37

key performance indicator (KPI) 91, 103
    definition 121

language
    clear 12
    see also wording discipline
lessons learned 61, 89, 109
lifecycle, definition 121
lines of reporting 76

managers, views about change 21, 22
Managing Successful Programmes (MSP), definition 121
    see also MSP
mapping
    importance 79–80
    types 80–4
mapping score *see* scoring
measure monitor
    definition 121
    role and responsibilities 73, 90
measurement
    purpose 89
    responsibility for 94
    spreading the load 56
measures
    appropriate criteria 91–2
    attributes and categories 40, 90–1
    baseline and predictions 45–6
    cost and difficulty 93–4
    definition 66, 89, 121
    determining 12
    identifying 36–7
metrics 12, 37, 66, 89, 90, 91, 92
    definition 122
milestone, definition 122
mind maps 29
mission
    achieving 3
    definition 122
    see also goal
MSP 17, 97, 104, 111, 112

net present value, definition 122

objectives
   appropriate number 21, 22
   defining and mapping 21–4
   definition 122
   linking to a vision 25
   setting 15, 16
OGC Gateway process 13, 18
opponents, including in workshops 28
optimization 54–5
   definition 122
organization
   appetite for risk 103, 104
   change lifecycle 104
   cultural change 10, 104, 105, 108, 111
   embedding BRM 108–10
   governance 104
   strategy and policies 105
   target future state 11
   vision/mission/values 3, 4, 104, 105

partial benefits map 69
personnel benefits 4
pet projects 4, 105
phase, definition 122
pilot projects 108
portfolio
   definition 122
   monitoring 104
   structure 107
portfolio balance 24, 26
   checking 50–4
   defining 74
portfolio board 21, 27, 39, 48
   definition 122
   role and responsibilities 61, 73–4, 105–6
portfolio management 73–4, 103–7
   consistent approach 108

   continuous/cyclical nature 104
   responsibility 105–6
Portfolio Management Guide (PfM) 103, 104, 107
portfolio management office (PMO), role and responsibilities 73, 105–6
portfolio office 73, 76
Portfolio, Programme and Project Offices (P3O) 105, 122
post-programme review 61
predicted value, definition 89, 122
PRINCE2 17, 97, 104
private sector 4, 6–7, 68, 108
programme board 49
   definition 123
   role and responsibilities 57, 61, 73, 74
programme brief 37–8
programme definition document (PDD) 44, 47–8
programme management 74–7
   definition 123
programme management office, role and responsibilities 73
programme manager 49, 56, 97
   role and responsibilities 22, 24, 47, 48, 57, 73, 111, 112, 113
programme office 76
programme team 49
   role and responsibilities 7, 94
programmes
   assessing 105
   boundary 24
   closure 61–2, 76, 104
   deciding what to include 42
   definition 122
   existing portfolio 21, 24
   possible structures 75, 78
   stakeholder engagement 13
   success or lack of it 8–9
progress, reporting 12
project board, role and responsibilities 73

project management 77
project management office, role and responsibilities 73
project manager, role and responsibilities 73, 76, 77
project team, role and limitations 7
projects
  cost reduction 9
  definition 123
  existing portfolio 21, 24
  stakeholder engagement 13
  success or lack of it 8–9

RAG status, definition 123
remedial action 17, 56, 61, 104
request for proposal (RFP) 43, 44
  definition 123
requirement definition process, definition 123
requirements
  detailed specification 43
  finalizing and costing 40–4
requirements definition 33–6
resistance to change see change(s)
resources
  definition 123
  mobilizing 49
  requirements 24, 27, 39, 56
results, documenting 28
return on investment (ROI)
  definition 123
  from benefit realization management 9, 108
  see also actual return on investment (AROI)
reviews 17–18, 61, 105
risk
  appetite for 103
  balance 104
risk register 27, 37
roll-out, time and sequence 55, 57
route maps see mapping

score, definition 123
scoring 42–3, 72, 84–8
senior responsible owner (SRO) 47, 49
  definition 123
  role and responsibilities 57, 73, 74
Sigma 6, 13, 111
Sigma value type classification 46, 51, 53, 67–9
sponsor
  definition 123
  responsibilities 22–4
stakeholder engagement
  challenging but essential 13
  continual 42
  in embedding BRM 18, 108
  maintaining 57
  in phase 4 50, 55
  plan 40
  strategy 37
  workshops 21, 28–9
stakeholder profile 40, 41
stakeholder representatives, resource requirements 39
stakeholders
  clustering 28–9
  definition 124
  engaging and involving see stakeholder engagement
  from the business community 48
  impact on 24
  key groups 16
  motivating 47
  multiple 7
  perceived disbenefits 33, 67
  reporting benefits to 61
  responsibility for measurement 94
statistical techniques 45
strategy map 22–4, 80, 82
  definition 124

success
   critical factors 14
   defining 10–11
   of programmes or projects 8–9

targets
   definition 89, 124
   missed 61
   negotiating 12
templates 97
terminology, definition 12
timescales, negotiating 12

UK government, emphasis on benefits 6

vision
   definition 124
   setting 15, 16
   see also goal
vision statement 11, 79
visual communication 12, 56, 65
   see also communication

weighted paths 42–3, 72, 84–8
   definition 124
'why' questions 21, 22, 65, 122
wish list 33, 80
wording discipline 65
workshops 21–4, 28
   British Council 111, 112

yield, definition 124
   see also return on investment (ROI)